feeding: solved

gurgle
.com

 # feeding: solved

Collins

First published in 2009 by
Collins, an imprint of
HarperCollins Publishers
77-85 Fulham Palace Road
London W6 8JB
www.collins.co.uk

A catalogue record for this book is available from the British Library

Project Editor: Corinne Roberts
Design: Heike Schüssler and Cooling Brown
Cover Design: Heike Schüssler

ISBN: 978 0 00 728917 2

Colour reproduction by Dot Gradations, Essex
Printed and bound in Hong Kong by Printing Express

Always seek the advice of your general practitioner or other qualified healthcare professional regarding any medical condition: the information given in this
book should not be treated as a substitute for professional medical advice.
Neither the author nor the publisher can be held responsible for any loss or
claim as a result of the use, or misuse, of the suggestions made or the failure
to take medical advice.

The contents of this book are correct at the time of going to print.

Contents

Foreword

The day after I gave birth to my first daughter, I was sitting in the maternity ward gazing adoringly at my tiny baby when the girl in the next bed, a second-time-around mum, leaned over and said, 'You should talk to your baby, you know, she'll love the sound of your voice and you haven't said anything to her yet. The more you speak to her, the quicker she'll learn to talk.' She was right. I was so busy admiring my new little bundle I hadn't uttered a word to her. I'd forgotten about my new role as her mum. From that moment on I plied the second-time-around-mum with the kind of questions I was too shy to ask the midwife: should my baby's legs be so curled up? Am I breastfeeding correctly? Are her fingers meant to be that purple and why am I so scared that something will happen to her if I go to the loo...

It was out of this constant need for answers that **gurgle.com** was born. I'm not the first mum who arrived home with a tiny baby feeling engulfed by the enormity of the task ahead. It didn't start there, the questions started before I became pregnant: what's ovulation? When will I fall pregnant? Will my morning sickness ever stop? At **gurgle.com** we try to provide parents and parents-to-be with a place they can visit for all those 3am worries, a place where they can see weekly updates of their child's development and above all a place where they can meet other parents going through exactly the same things they are. After all, having a baby is not a journey anyone should do alone.

The more we talked to the mums using **gurgle**, the more we realised that the same questions came up again and again. So we decided to publish a set of **gurgle** handbooks in response to the most asked questions on the site. We want these books to guide you through what mums have told us are the three trickiest areas of parenting: how to enjoy your pregnancy (and we promise you can), getting your baby into good sleep habits, and feeding your baby. We don't want to preach or tell you how it should be done, but we do want to provide you with lots of helpful information and tips based on the advice of both our **gurgle** panel of experts and our incredibly supportive and knowledgeable community of mums.

We want you to see our **gurgle** books as your older sister or best friend who has had a baby and is passing on her knowledge to you. We're the midwife who helps you with breastfeeding, or the auntie who suggests a way to help your baby sleep at night.

As much as I wanted to take my maternity ward 'neighbour' home with me, I couldn't. I had to learn how to become a parent, just as my daughter had to learn to sit, walk and talk. We hope that these books become that tap on the shoulder in the maternity ward giving you a friendly nudge in the right direction. Oh, and just for the record, my daughter is now a right little chatterbox...

Nifa McLaughlin
Editor of **gurgle.com** and mum to Ivy and Poppy

 We hope you enjoy our books and if we've missed anything out, please visit **gurgle.com** for lots more videos, groups, articles, chat and tools to complement these books. Register with **gurgle.com** and receive free weekly emails walking you through pregnancy and parenthood.

Choosing to breastfeed

Breastfeeding: the lowdown

If you choose to breastfeed, you can be sure your baby will be receiving literally all he needs to grow and thrive during the first six months of his life. Manufacturers of formula milk and artificial substitutes have spent years trying to reproduce the marvellous qualities of breast milk but, so far, nobody has quite managed to emulate the mass of nutrients found in it. On the other hand, there are many reasons why a woman may not be able to breastfeed, and if that applies to you, don't torment yourself with guilt about it, as your baby will still receive all the nutritional benefit he needs from formula milk.

The difference between formula and breast milk is that the latter is a 'live' liquid, full of antibodies which help fight against infections that might come your baby's way, as well as containing active cells which work to soak up viruses and any bacteria that might come into contact with your baby. So, even if you breastfed only once after the birth and then went on to feed him formula milk, your baby will still have received a dose of antibodies from you.

As well as boosting and supporting your baby's immature immune system, breast milk has the great advantage that it is always available fresh and at the right temperature. The skin-to-skin contact that a breastfed baby has with his mother can provide an important part of the bonding process, although there is no reason why a bottlefed baby cannot have the same contact with his mother. Additionally, breastfeeding is very convenient, does not cost a penny (although your own appetite may well go up, with cost implications there!) and, with no packaging or transportation issues, is good for the environment too.

Why breast is best

Studies have shown that breastfed babies and children are far less likely to suffer from various illnesses both in the short term and in later life. These include prolonged colds, allergies, eczema, a five times higher risk of diarrhoea and vomiting (requiring hospital admission), insulin-dependent diabetes, heart disease, obesity, ear and urinary tract infections, and severe respiratory infections – to name but a few. Children who are not breastfed are also at greater risk of obesity and high blood pressure in later years, and show lower than average scores on tests of neurological development. Breastfeeding benefits the mother too: as well as helping you get your figure back more quickly, it can reduce the risk of osteoporosis, breast cancer and cancer of the ovaries.

How it works

Regardless of your breast shape or size (even if you are as flat as a pancake!), be reassured that your breasts will be able to do the job they were intended for. It is a myth that women with big breasts will be 'better' at breastfeeding. They may have more fatty tissue inside their breasts, but fat does not have a function as far as breastfeeding is concerned. Anatomically speaking, all lactating breasts perform in the same way.

Milk-producing cells throughout the breast create milk that is stored in little sacs called alveoli. These sacs feed into ducts (each breast has around 20 of these) that open into the nipple area and release milk when your baby sucks.

During pregnancy, it is likely that your breasts underwent some changes. The skin around your nipple (the areola) containing the Montgomery glands (visible as small bumps) and hair follicles may well have darkened in colour, and hair may have become more noticeable around the nipple. You may also have noticed prominent blue veins appearing under the surface of the skin of each breast. After your baby is born, these work to establish a good blood supply to your breasts to aid milk production.

All of the above doesn't mean that your bottlefed baby is going to be sickly, but breastfed babies do have the best start, which is why it is good to try to breastfeed even just once or twice when your baby is newborn, as this will help to make a positive difference. While some women are genuinely unable to breastfeed – due to illness, for instance – others choose not to breastfeed because they believe they are not able to. This is generally not the case, however, and, with the right support and guidance, you will be able to breastfeed. It is only a small minority of women who are unable to do so. (For advice on how to breastfeed correctly, see pages 18–23.)

If you're worried about not being able to go back to work or cope with being the only person able to feed your baby, it's a good idea to consider the possibility of supplementing breastfeeding by expressing milk that can then be given in a bottle to your baby. It is possible to express milk while you are at work provided you have a fridge in which to store it during the day. This means that other people can share the responsibility of feeding and your baby will be easier to wean off the breast when the time comes. Babies that are exclusively breastfed often take longer to wean. (For advice on expressing milk, by hand or using a pump, see pages 32–5.)

Despite the huge benefits of breastfeeding and despite all the endorsement of it by the medical profession, the UK has one of the lowest breastfeeding rates in Europe. A third of British women never try to breastfeed, compared to a tiny 2% of women in Sweden. If you are having problems, please seek advice from your midwife or health visitor, as they can usually be solved with a little help.

Support for breastfeeding

One of the reasons why the breastfeeding rate in the UK is so low may be due to the fact that we don't have a culture that supports it, unlike other parts of the world. It is very important that women who want to breastfeed have support from the people around them: their family, friends and work colleagues. And they should feel that breastfeeding outside the home is acceptable. In reality, many women feel intimidated or uncomfortable about the prospect of breastfeeding in public. This shouldn't be the case, however: society should be more encouraging of it, so that women no longer feel so awkward or embarrassed.

Feeding your baby is a necessity – not a luxury – and should be treated as such. Leaving the house with a new baby can seem like a military operation and the last thing you want to worry about is not knowing whether you'll be able to feed your baby when you're out and about. Mums should be able to breastfeed whenever and wherever; every public place should have a special mother and baby feeding room, as most women prefer some privacy while breastfeeding. Attitudes need to change in society and for this to happen, places of work, public institutions and eating places should adopt a friendlier approach to breastfeeding.

Research has shown that nine out of ten women who stop breastfeeding in the first six weeks give up before they want to. Hence many mums and babies are missing out on the benefits of breastfeeding simply because some people and certain establishments are still not well disposed towards it.

It's true that there has been considerable improvement in people's attitudes in the past few years: a recent poll showed that 84% of adults don't object to women breastfeeding in public. However, some individuals clearly still feel uncomfortable when they see a woman breastfeeding, maybe viewing it as something sexual.

Lots of useful advice on the subject can be found through the charity organization the National Childbirth Trust. This offers support to breastfeeding women while encouraging friends, relations and partners of women to support breastfeeding too. If you feel that you need help, advice or encouragement, either for yourself or somebody else, then you can call the NCT breastfeeding line, open 8am–10pm every day and manned by trained breastfeeding counsellors who can help you (see 'Resources', pages 216–17, for contact details).

Mum's top tip

I would recommend that you give breastfeeding a go to start with. Your body will naturally produce enough milk so your baby will definitely be getting enough food. My son was a bit fussy at first and I soon found out the reason for this was wind (I'd heard that breastfed babies don't get wind but they most certainly do!). My son is 19 weeks now and feeding well and at the same time every day. Keep trying, you will crack it in the end.

All about breast milk

From around six months of pregnancy, your breasts produce a substance called colostrum, which is the early milk your body makes – super-rich in proteins and antibodies – ready for your baby's first drink. Colostrum aids the passing of meconium (the sticky, black stools that your baby expels in her first few days of life).

According to the National Childbirth Trust, feeding your baby colostrum in those early days will enable her to avoid jaundice, as colostrum helps her expel bilirubin (an orange pigment) from her bowels. Colostrum, which is slightly yellowish in appearance, is also crucial for passing on valuable nutrients and antibodies to help kickstart your baby's immune system. This milk lasts for only three to four days after your baby is born (and as there aren't huge amounts, feeds will be shorter in those early days), after which your full milk comes in.

It is very important to get good advice on breastfeeding at this early stage. The main reason why it tends not to go well, or is quickly abandoned, is due to bad positioning of the baby at the breast (causing chafed, sore nipples, and frustration for both mother and child) and a lack of support from the people who could make a real difference at this stage – namely, midwives and other carers. If you can make it work now, you and your baby will both feel the benefits later on. (For advice on breastfeeding correctly, see pages 18–23.)

After the colostrum has been used up, your milk comes in; you will know because your breasts will become bigger and fuller. There are two different types of milk that your baby will be drinking: fore and hind milk. Fore milk, which is what your baby takes when she first latches on, is thirst-quenching and more diluted than the hind milk that follows. Thicker and full of calories, this is the stuff that makes your child really grow and develop. Once breastfeeding is established, you will need to swap breasts for your baby to feed on so that she receives as much hind milk as possible.

It is important once your milk does come in that your breasts are regularly emptied in order to stimulate and ensure a good supply of milk. Your baby will probably need to take anything from six to nine feeds daily at first; this will mean feeding her around every three to four hours. If she is feeding more than this, you will both become very tired and you should try to make her take bigger feeds so that she needs to be fed less frequently.

The more you feed, the higher your prolactin (the hormone which triggers milk production) levels will be, and the higher these are, the more milk you will produce. If you let your baby decide when she needs to be fed, your body will work out how much milk is going to be enough for her. You will not run out of milk, rest assured!

Human breast milk does look different from other milk. It can be thin and watery and have a blue or yellow tinge to it, or even a hint of green or orange, depending on what the mother has been eating. This is perfectly normal, so don't be surprised if it's not quite what you expected.

Breastfeeding correctly

It might surprise you to learn that breastfeeding is a skill that has to be learnt and that just brandishing a nipple near your baby's mouth won't necessarily get the whole thing going. But it's well worth persevering: once you have a few basic skills under your belt (or bra), you'll find it a very rewarding experience. Often, though, women feel frustrated and upset because they have found breastfeeding very difficult to master, mainly due to a lack of support and sensible advice. The really important thing is not to give up.

Admittedly, breastfeeding is not always a piece of cake from the start, but on the positive side, that is usually only due to some minor adjustments needing to be made. Once these have been sorted out, you'll be breastfeeding smoothly and happily.

Some babies (and mums) take to it easily and others find it far more difficult. If you have the right support from your partner, healthcare providers and family or friends, you are going to find it a whole lot easier.

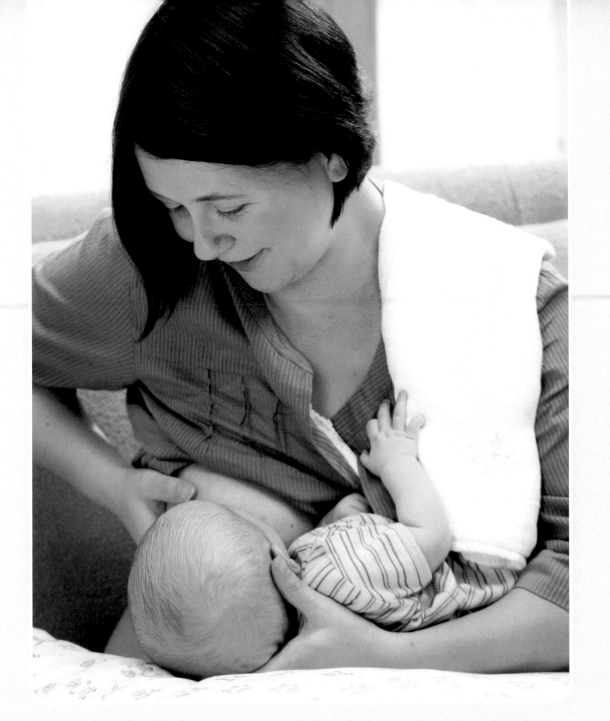

Latching on

To begin with, what's important to understand is that your baby won't feed properly if he's not 'latched on' correctly. He may know instinctively how to latch on to your breast, especially if he's been positioned properly, but if he is at an awkward angle in relation to your breast then he will probably find it very hard. Bear in mind, too, that some shapes of breast may make it more of a challenge for the inexperienced baby to latch on to properly. Whatever the reason, your baby may become frustrated because he is not receiving the milk he needs to fill up his tummy. Meanwhile, you may be experiencing sore nipples and other discomfort. (See page 17 for advice on how often to feed your baby.)

The correct positioning of your baby to your breast is the key to it all. What most new mums don't realize is that a baby needs more than just the nipple in his mouth. In addition to your nipple, he'll need to have all or most of the areola (the dark skin surrounding the nipple) in his mouth, depending on the size of your areola, of course. This means he will be latched on to quite a big section of your breast. The clamp of his jaws over this whole area, combined with the pull of his sucking, should mean that he can access the area behind the nipple where the milk is stored.

His nose should be touching the skin of your breast. Don't worry that he'll suffocate; if he is having trouble breathing, he'll let you know about it. Besides, this is what he was designed to do in order to survive. It would be a bit strange if babies were put under any risk through doing the thing that ensures their survival! If your baby is latched on properly, his lower lip should be pulled slightly back, with the tongue positioned underneath, rather than above, the nipple itself. In addition, his mouth should be level with the nipple, which should go straight into his mouth without bending. The best way to achieve this is to lay your baby on your lap, positioning him on his side and propping him up underneath with a couple of pillows to ensure he's at the right height in relation to your breast.

Before I breastfeed, I always make sure I change my baby's nappy so that when he falls asleep he won't wake again soon after with an uncomfortably full or wet nappy. It's good practice to get a nappy-changing routine going anyway. Of course, he might only dirty his nappy after I've fed him, so if he does stay asleep I don't change him until he wakes again.

Breastfeeding positions – dos and don'ts

- **Do** make sure you are sitting in a comfortable position with your back well supported by cushions or the back of a chair.

- **Do** ensure your baby's head is level with your breast. If this is difficult, prop him up by placing some pillows or cushions underneath him.

- **Do** make sure your baby lies with his tummy against yours, as this is the easiest position for successful feeding.

- **Do** make sure the nipple is straight and level with his mouth. The best way to do this is to align your baby's head so his nose is level with your nipple. This ensures he will open up his mouth and 'root' (search) for the nipple.

- **Don't** leave a gap between your breast and your baby's mouth. Make sure he is touching your breast with his nose.

- **Don't** allow his tongue to go over your nipple. It should be underneath.

- **Don't** hold his head as babies don't like it!

top tips

Breastfeeding: a seven-step summary

1 To get your baby ready for breastfeeding, first change his nappy if it's dirty and make sure the room is warm.

2 Prepare for feeding by choosing a comfortable place to sit, preferably on a sofa or chair with your back fully supported with cushions. Have a big glass of water to hand, plus a cloth to clean up any possetted milk and perhaps something to help occupy the time, such as a book or the radio.

3 Next, it's crucial to get your baby into a good position. In the early days, the best way of doing this is to have your baby lying stomach to stomach with you, and raised up to the height of your breasts with a pillow or two underneath him. His head should be supported by your arm but not held in your hand.

4 When your baby's face is parallel to your breast, the nipple should be level with his nose. He will then root (use his search instinct) to find your nipple with his mouth.

5 When your baby has located your nipple (help him if he needs you to), he should take the whole nipple and most of the skin (areola) behind the nipple before he starts sucking. This is called being 'latched on'. If he is doing this correctly, you shouldn't feel any pain and your baby's jaw nearest his ear should move up and down as he sucks. If you do feel pain, then you need to reposition your baby. His nose should touch the skin of your breast.

6 When your breast feels emptier, it's time to change breasts, so that your baby can receive more fore and hind milk from the other one.

7 Start feeding your baby from the breast you last fed on. This means each breast will receive the right amount of stimulation to ensure a good milk supply. It will also ensure your baby receives the highly nutritious fatty hind milk from both breasts. To help you remember which breast you should be feeding your baby from next, you could pop a bracelet around the corresponding wrist or tie a ribbon onto the appropriate side of your bra.

Mum's top tip

The best advice I was given was to invest in three or four good feeding bras. The right support for your breasts is essential while breastfeeding because an ill-fitting bra can lead to problems such as blocked ducts and mastitis. I also bought a couple of special breastfeeding tops that were sensitively designed in order to give as much privacy as possible. A shawl or big scarf can also help protect your modesty if you are planning on feeding in public.

What's safe to eat while breastfeeding

The range of foods to avoid while pregnant can sometimes look worryingly like your weekly shopping list. Nice, juicy, rare steak? How about some fresh tuna? Bottle of red? Bit of Brie to follow? And to finish, what better than a strong espresso? Ha! No chance. Even the humble egg has to be cooked to the point where it could give a rock a run for its money before being allowed to pass your lips. And where's the fun in that?

So, when you finally pop the little one out, can you gorge yourself on all those things that you've been strictly avoiding for the last 40 or so weeks? Well... you'd like to think so. But if you're breastfeeding, some restrictions still apply.

Shopping for a hungry mum

Happily, it's not such a strict list. It's more of a common sense one. The best thing, for yourself and for your baby, is to eat a healthy, balanced diet. It'll keep your energy levels up too. Avoiding too many sugary snacks and treats can also prevent any crashing sugar 'lows'. You might find you're more susceptible to these when you've just had a baby – your hormones can be all over the shop and rationality flies out of the window. It's probably best to get other people to help with the shopping – for a couple of reasons. Firstly, the thought of traipsing round a supermarket when you've just had a baby will be enough to make you cry, and secondly, you'll probably just come back with all the things you tried to avoid during the previous 40 weeks. And there won't be much room in the back of your car for food when it's already filled with 34 bottles of wine and an industrial-sized pack of breast pads!

What's allowed and what isn't

SOFT CHEESE
If you're a fan of soft cheese, then rejoice – you're allowed it again! Although listeria (which is the reason you steer clear of soft cheese and unpasteurized products during pregnancy) has been found in breast milk, it isn't passed to the feeding child.

PEANUTS
Some health experts suggest avoiding peanuts if there is a history of peanut allergy in you or your partner's family. This will avoid sensitizing your baby. (For advice on food allergies and allergic reactions, see pages 162–9.)

ALCOHOL
There is no hard evidence to suggest that drinking the odd glass of wine while breastfeeding is harmful to your baby. But if you really don't want to pass any alcohol on to your child, then abstain completely.

CAFFEINE
Caffeine could disturb your baby's sleep patterns. If you really can't do without caffeine after being so good for so long, then time your cuppa so it's a couple of hours before the next feed, or express beforehand so there's no chance of passing it on through your milk. As with alcohol, stick to moderate amounts rather than going crazy in Starbucks the moment the cord is cut. It's a bit of a vicious circle, as you're so tired initially that you probably feel a greater need for tea or coffee, but the more you have, the more you may disrupt your baby's sleep patterns. (See overleaf for more on this.)

FISH
It's recommended that you avoid certain fish (shark, swordfish and marlin – which, to be honest, don't appear in that many

people's shopping baskets) because of the high levels of mercury they contain. It's also wise to not eat more than two portions of oily fish a week – trout, mackerel, sardines and fresh tuna. Canned tuna is fine.

The diet starts tomorrow

Don't try to lose weight while breastfeeding. Although you might be in despair at the fact you look no different to when you were 40 weeks pregnant, if you're breastfeeding you need all the energy you can get. And you'll get it from food. You need 1,800 calories a day to produce enough milk, and if you're losing more than 0.5–2kg (1–4lb) a month, you're probably not eating enough. However, if you were overweight before getting pregnant, or put on a lot of weight during pregnancy, you can probably afford to lose between 2 and 3kg (4 and 6lb) a month without damaging your milk production. But this is not the time to embrace a strict diet.

Keep your energy levels high

Eat plenty of calcium-rich food, such as cheese, yoghurt and good-quality ice cream (yes, really!). Drink milk and plenty of water, and up your intake of protein: meat, poultry, eggs, tofu, beans and nuts are all good sources. Starchy carbohydrates such as pasta, bread and potatoes will also help keep your energy levels up. And, as always, try to eat plenty of fresh fruit and veg. Now, this might seem a lot, and what with feeding your new baby and getting enough to eat yourself, you'll probably feel as if all you're doing is thinking about food. But after a couple of weeks, the simple matter of eating well will become less of a chore, and you'll find yourself not thinking about it so much – it'll have become second nature.

How caffeine affects breast milk

If you are breastfeeding, you are sure to feel thirsty and also perhaps a little tired. Both these factors can make you crave tea or coffee. While it's fine to have either in moderation, if you are drinking more than a couple of cups of coffee a day, there may be a negative impact you should consider.

Bear in mind that caffeine is a drug and if you are breastfeeding, it will cross into your baby's milk. If you can help it, it's probably not a good idea to expose her to it as it may make her restless and irritable. It may also disturb her sleep patterns and have an adverse effect on any bedtime routine you may have established. For this reason, it's best to limit your caffeine intake.

Apart from anything, caffeine may make your breast milk taste or smell different, which can make your baby fuss at the breast, or in the worst case, it could upset her stomach and cause diarrhoea. Similarly, if you are drinking too much caffeine, you may find yourself getting more jittery and on edge.

Most GPs will err on the side of caution and tell you to avoid caffeine or cut back on your intake if you are trying to conceive, during pregnancy or while breastfeeding. Try to limit your coffee consumption to about 300mg per day (about 2–3 cups of coffee).

Caffeine is found naturally in tea, coffee and chocolate and is added to cola drinks, energy drinks and over-the-counter products. Quantities of caffeine vary from product to product, so always check the labels first. Don't forget that caffeine can even be found in some headache, cold and flu remedies! This doesn't mean avoiding them altogether but it does mean cutting back. If you suffer from caffeine withdrawal symptoms, cut back slowly, or fill your cup halfway with coffee and the other half with milk. Gradually you will be able to cut caffeine out of your diet altogether.

It is important to drink plenty of fluids when you are breastfeeding, but it is essential to drink the right kind of fluids. Water is most definitely best, followed by herbal or fruit teas and fresh juices.

Mum's top tip

Now that my baby's in a fairly regular feeding routine I find that breastfeeding can get very boring, so I put the time to good use by catching up on novels and films. I know from friends with older children that there'll come a time, running around after a hyperactive toddler, when I'll miss the quiet relaxation of breastfeeding and I'd recommend you make the most of it while you can too!

Safe medicines and ones to avoid

When you're a new parent, lacking sleep and feeling crabby and run-down, you're a prime candidate for a throbbing headache. Usually, you'd just open the medicine cabinet, but when you're breastfeeding you have to think about what painkiller you're taking. Always check with your pharmacist for your own peace of mind before taking any over-the-counter medicines while you are breastfeeding.

- Any medicine containing aspirin is to be avoided as it may be passed to your baby through your milk. There's a risk of a condition called Reyes syndrome occurring (a life-threatening metabolic disorder), which could affect your child if he is exposed to aspirin at a young age. For this reason, it's best to steer clear of all products containing aspirin.

- Codeine is another one to miss. Studies indicate that the children of breastfeeding mothers taking codeine show adverse effects, including poor feeding, low heart rate, tiredness, lack of energy and trouble breathing. If you are suffering from a headache and low-dose painkillers aren't working, always speak to a doctor before trying anything stronger.

- Ibuprofen is an anti-inflammatory and can be taken while breastfeeding, but only for a short time. Always check products for ingredients as some ibuprofen items also contain codeine to make them stronger.

- Paracetamol is safe on its own, but, again, check the packet to see if anything else is included. Some products may also contain aspirin or codeine.

- Some 'fast-acting' medicines (they will usually have an 'extra' or 'plus' in the name) also contain caffeine. So if you're trying to avoid it in your daily diet, you might want to check before taking it in a tablet.

- Many cold and flu remedies contain a mixture of drugs. Speak to the pharmacist and explain your symptoms; always tell her that you're breastfeeding. If you've sent someone else out to the chemist (and to be honest, that's what you should do!), ensure he or she mentions that you are nursing. If possible, write a note describing all of your symptoms so there can be no misunderstanding.

- If you've got a stuffed-up nose, then a totally harmless way of treating it is using an inhalant. A certain type of decongestant drug called pseudoephedrine can lead to decreased milk production, however, and so is best avoided.

- Some cough and cold medicines contain diphenhydramine and promethazine. These are used to dry up a runny nose and aid sleep. Now, although that might seem like a dream to you, unfortunately it'll be passed to your child through your milk and may make him drowsy. This, in turn, could lead to him feeding less and not gaining weight fast enough.

Safe medicines and ones to avoid

Expressing breast milk

Expressing milk just describes the process by which you take milk out of your breasts to put in a bottle for your baby. If you're thinking of leaving your baby with other people, even if that possibility seems far in the future, it's definitely worth getting used to expressing breast milk.

This means that you will be able to leave your baby for a longer period than just the few hours in between feeds – essential if you plan on going back to work in the early months after giving birth. To this end, introducing him to a bottle, if you are breastfeeding, is actually a good idea. However, it is not recommended you start expressing until you have established a good breastfeeding routine with your baby.

Mum's top tip

My health visitor advised me not start expressing until I'd got a good breastfeeding routine going with my baby, at around six weeks after the birth. Once I was ready to start, I expressed by hand or using a breast pump. I found the best time to do this was directly following a feed, in order to fully drain my breasts. Usually, I had most milk in the morning, so I expressed after the first feed of the day.

Make sure all necessary equipment is sterilized properly and express some milk (see overleaf). Wait until your baby is hungry for a feed before trying to give him the bottle. If you put some of your breast milk on the teat, he will probably accept it. If he takes a dummy, that may also make things a little easier. If you are having problems getting your baby to take a bottle, ask for help and advice from your health visitor.

 For the **gurgle** video on **Sterilizing your feeding equipment**, go to **gurgle.com** and click on **Videos**

When to express breast milk

It's best to express milk directly after a feed, to give your breasts time to fill up again. You may find you have most milk in the morning, and hence that's a good time to express, but you will obviously need to find out what suits you and your busy routine best. If you don't seem to have much milk in your breasts after a feed, just try later. The essential thing is to relax and not worry too much as your body will respond accordingly.

If you are not going to be expressing milk frequently, you may want to try expressing by hand – a cheaper, yet possibly slightly trickier method. Warm your breasts first – have a bath or put a warm, damp flannel over them – then massage them a little before you begin. This will make hand expressing a bit easier.

 For the **gurgle** video on **Pumping and expressing milk**, go to **gurgle.com** and click on **Videos**

Top tips for expressing breast milk

1 Have a sterile bottle or container to hold the milk. Start by thinking about your baby – the idea is to stimulate your 'let-down' reflex, which lets your body know it's time for your baby to feed and your milk to start flowing.

2 Next, try repeatedly squeezing and releasing the areola behind the nipple. You should see milk appear on the nipple, which, if you lean forward and continue to squeeze, will squirt out in jets. Don't worry if it doesn't seem as if you are getting much milk. It may be your breasts are relatively empty or you might just have a slow flow. Even if you manage only a little, you can always come back later to try a bit more.

3 Do change breasts, especially if your flow seems slow on one side; it may be that one breast is carrying more milk. Little and often is the advice offered by the National Childbirth Trust (NCT), who recommend expressing every three hours for ten minutes, aiming for a total of six to eight sessions over 24 hours.

4 You can also collect breast milk from one breast with a breast shell whilst feeding from the other, as your let-down reflex is active in both breasts when you feed.

5 If hand expressing doesn't appeal to you, or you're finding it difficult, you may find an electric breast pump is the answer. You can hire these from the NCT (see 'Resources', pages 216–17, for contact details), or, if you are planning on using the pump a lot or having more children, you may want to purchase one to keep. You can buy these at all good chemists or baby shops.

Breast pumps have detailed instructions demonstrating how to assemble the parts and how to position the pump on your breast. It shouldn't be painful if you are doing it properly and follow the equipment notes carefully. Just as when you were first learning to breastfeed your baby, positioning is everything. If you are having difficulties, ask for help from your health visitor or a breastfeeding counsellor.

top tips

Storing breast milk safely

- Store breast milk in the fridge or freezer in sterilized bottles, labelling the bottle with the date the milk was expressed.

- Refrigerate promptly after expressing and use within two days, or freeze and use within two weeks.

- Throw away any unused breast milk which may be left in the bottle after a feed.

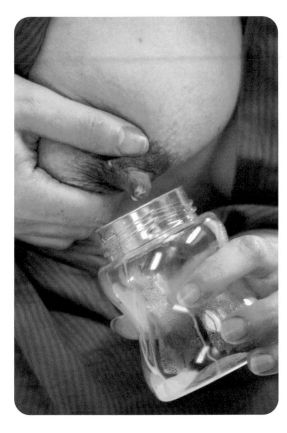
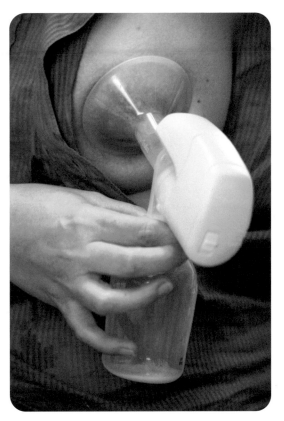

Breastfeeding a premature baby

Having a baby earlier than planned can be an enormous shock, and caring for your newborn in the first few months will probably be very different from how you imagined, especially if he is admitted to a neonatal unit. The good news is that you can still do many of the things you originally planned, including breastfeeding, even if your baby is born very early.

Breast milk is great for your baby, offering protection against germs through your own antibodies. It is also easier for babies to tolerate than formula milk and provides all the nutrients and nourishment they need to grow and develop. A mother's milk is especially valuable for premature babies because their immune systems are weak. It helps boost their defences against illness, while the growth factors it contains encourage them to develop in those all important first few months.

If your baby has been born very early, he may not be ready to feed directly from your breast straight away. He might have to be fed through a drip to start with, particularly if there are breathing difficulties. From there he can progress to breast milk, which is most likely to be fed to him via a tiny tube that will go through his nose and into his stomach. With supervision from the nurses, it may be possible for you to help with tube-feeding your baby. This can help you bond with your baby as well as showing you how much he is benefiting from your milk.

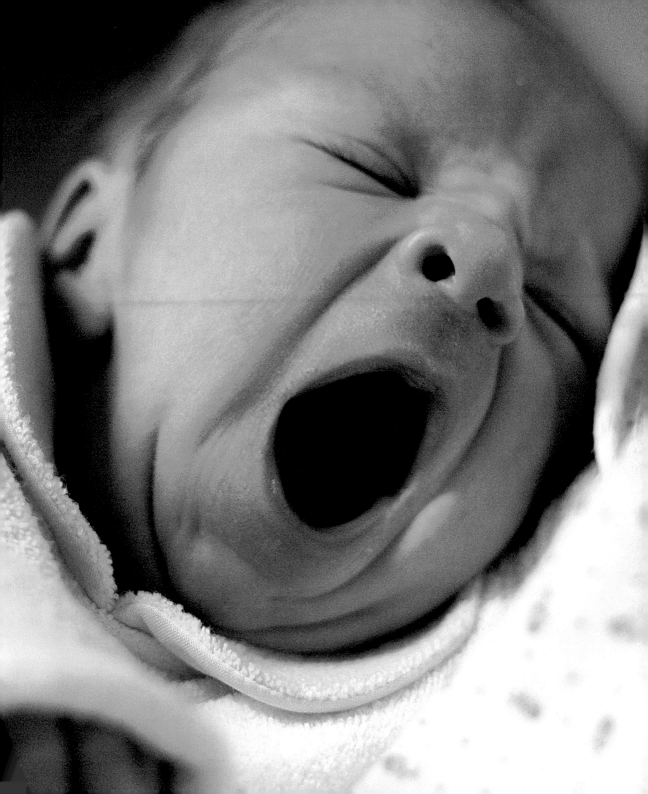

Expressing milk for a premature baby

To enable your baby to be tube-fed, you will need to collect your milk by expressing it. When your baby suckles at your breast, it stimulates the milk ducts, and expressing mimics that suckling motion. It's a skill that takes time to learn and there are a number of different methods that can be used, from electrical pumps to expressing by hand. The staff that are looking after your baby will give you all the advice, support and help you need if you decide you want to start expressing for your baby. (For more information on how to express, see pages 32–5.)

Having to express milk can sometimes feel like a extra pressure at an already stressful and emotional time. However, it is important to remember that no matter how much or little you are able to express, your baby will benefit.

Kangaroo care

As soon as your baby's condition becomes stable, you may be encouraged to practise 'kangaroo' care, which means holding and cuddling your naked baby next to your skin, like a young kangaroo in its mother's pouch. Being placed skin-to-skin will build your maternal bond, make your baby feel warm and secure and gradually prepare him for breastfeeding. Close contact like this also helps stimulate your body to produce milk, and encourages your immune system to make more antibodies, which will transfer through your breast milk to your baby and protect him against infection.

Eventually, when your baby is developed enough, you will be able to feed him directly from your breast. When you first put him on your breast, don't worry if he doesn't suckle; he'll still benefit from being close to you, enjoying the taste and smell of the milk expressed onto your nipple. At the first feed, don't expect too much, since premature babies get tired easily and must gradually learn to suck.

To avoid tiring your baby, massage your breasts first (your healthcare team will advise you on how to do this) and then express a little milk onto the nipple before putting him to the breast. Remember to move him towards the breast rather than your breast towards him. It's a good idea to use pillows to support you and to raise your baby so that he is level with the breast to encourage him to feed (see pages 18–23).

Helping your baby learn to suckle

Many hospitals also promote ways of helping babies learn to suck. Your unit may provide soothers (dummies) suitable for premature babies to suckle on while being tube-fed, or recommend dry breastfeeding, which involves you expressing your milk to be tube-fed to your baby and then allowing your baby to suckle on your emptied breast. Either technique will help your baby learn to associate sucking with a full stomach.

Breastfeeding your premature baby is a big commitment, which will need dedication, encouragement and support from everyone involved. It will test you physically and emotionally but it can be extremely rewarding. By breastfeeding you are giving your newborn something very valuable – a good start early in life and the best chance of growing into a healthy, happy child.

For further information about breastfeeding premature babies or any advice on looking after your premature baby, you can call the free BLISS helpline or log onto the BLISS website (see 'Resources', pages 216–17, for contact details).

Sleep and breastfeeding

Depending on the way you approach sleep for your breastfed baby, there is really no reason why you should not get a good night-time routine going. Something that is generally frowned upon is breastfeeding your baby until she falls asleep. The reason for this is that she should be able to sleep without 'sleep associations' or 'cues' like your breast.

If you feed your baby to sleep every night, you may be storing trouble for yourself as every night she will expect to be breastfed to sleep. She will not be able to sleep without the comfort of your breast, which could mean you are the only person able to comfort her when she wakes in the early hours. It could also mean that she's merely suckling on the breast and not really taking in enough milk to keep her satisfied.

Some people suggest that your baby should be fully awake when you feed her. If your baby is particularly sleepy while feeding and keeps drifting off, it might be worth breaking the pattern by changing her nappy or walking round the room with her, so that she's then sufficiently awake to finish her feed and doesn't wake up two hours later hungry for more!

Some mothers disagree that feeding their babies to sleep every night is a bad thing, and are happy to establish this routine. This is a matter of personal preference, of course. Indeed, if, for example, you are co-sleeping with your baby, breastfeeding can actually be a wonderful bonding time that hardly disturbs your night anyway.

Alternatively, if your baby will take a bottle, your partner could give her the night-time feed with some expressed milk, thus ensuring you are not the only person leaping around after midnight and giving you the opportunity to catch up on some sleep. You will learn what works best for you and your baby.

Breastfeeding twins

Although a little daunting, rest assured that it is both possible and sustainable to breastfeed twin babies. Your body can produce enough milk for two, and as twins are more likely to be born prematurely, they will especially benefit from the protective goodness of breast milk. In addition, breastfeeding twins is going to help you save time, as preparing bottles for two will be very time-consuming.

If your babies are born prematurely, they are likely to be fed by a tube (see pages 36–9). If they are born at approximately 37 weeks, they may have problems in getting milk from your breast, as they don't normally have a mature sucking reflex. If this is the case, then feed them expressed milk from a special feeding cup (rather than a bottle, which might make a transition to breast later more difficult) and change over to the breast when they are ready.

Finding a routine that fits

At first, it may be easier to feed one baby at a time, but it is possible to feed simultaneously, if that makes things easier for you. Trying to impose a feeding schedule on twins is likely to be difficult, especially at first. Either feeding on demand (which will help to establish the correct milk supply for your babies) or letting one baby wake to feed and then waking the other so they start to feed at the same time, is probably the best option.

You are likely to be ravenously hungry, so don't miss meals if possible and ensure you have plenty of snacks to hand to keep your blood-sugar levels stable. Make sure you drink lots of water, too, as it will be easy for you to get dehydrated.

Your babies may well have a preference about which breast they feed from. If they are similar weights, this is fine. However, if one twin is larger, it's a good idea to alternate so that both breasts are stimulated to produce a good supply of milk.

Breastfeeding position with twins

If you're feeding your twins at the same time, you'll need to think of how to position them. You could adopt the 'traditional' position (see pages 18–23), with one lying in front of the other. Or you could try what is known (rather unceremoniously!) as the 'football hold'.

To do this, you tuck one of your babies under each arm, with one hand supporting each head, so that their feet are extending beyond your back. You'll need to be sitting up (in bed is fine), with pillows supporting your back so that you're leaning forward a little. You could vary this, of course, and have one baby in the football hold, while the other is in the traditional feeding position.

Obviously, it is worth experimenting to find what works best for you and your babies. In the early days, it's also a good idea to ask your partner to lend a hand while you're getting the hang of it.

Mum's top tip

When breastfeeding twins, my advice is to wind them after every feed, so they are not uncomfortable afterwards. All babies take in some air as they feed (although it's usually more of a problem with bottle-fed babies), so it's important to wind your babies even if they've fallen asleep. And don't become dehydrated while breastfeeding – make sure you always have a glass of water to hand. It's thirsty work for all three of you.

Postnatal breast problems

If you are breastfeeding (or even if you don't end up breastfeeding), there are various issues that may affect you that you should be aware of. If you are having problems that are affecting your ability to breastfeed, you should definitely talk to your health visitor or local breastfeeding counsellor before giving up. Most problems can be remedied and you can continue breastfeeding with confidence.

What you should remember is that if your baby is latched on properly, you shouldn't be experiencing any pain. It is important to get your breastfeeding position properly established otherwise your baby may be unable to feed and you may find the start of the feed very painful and traumatic. (For advice on this, see pages 18–23.)

Below are some of the common conditions that can make breastfeeding difficult, with advice on how to address them.

Sore and cracked nipples

Breastfeeding with sore and cracked nipples can be really painful. Don't suffer in silence, ask your health visitor or breastfeeding counsellor for help if you're struggling. If you have sore nipples, this is usually because your baby is not latched on properly to your breast. Other causes can be: longer than usual feeding times (again usually due to bad breastfeeding position); a skin problem such as thrush; or, more rarely, a circulatory problem known as 'white nipple'. Whatever the cause, your nipples may be cracked, bleeding, bruised-looking or generally tender. And you are likely to find that feeding gets more and more painful.

Usually nipples go through a toughening-up period when you first start feeding but, of course, if you are experiencing pain you should consult your GP or health visitor. You may be advised to use a nipple shield for a while, and there are creams available to soothe and help heal the nipples. Make sure that your baby is latched on properly and you should find that the problem clears up.

Engorged breasts

This happens when the milk comes in too fast or you are over-producing. It normally occurs during the first few days of breastfeeding. If your baby is not latching on correctly and therefore not emptying the breast, this can cause it to become swollen. Missing out on night feeds can add to the problem.

The only viable solution to this is to try and empty your breasts as fully as possible. Use a breast pump if necessary (see page 34). Some women swear by cold cabbage leaves in their bra, which help to reduce the heat and swelling that accompanies engorged breasts. A mild painkiller such as paracetamol can be taken if you are in great discomfort, but watch out: if the engorgement is not addressed, you could get mastitis (see overleaf).

Blocked milk ducts

If you feel tiny lumps in your breast, it could indicate that some milk ducts are blocked. If your breasts are swollen and engorged, this is more likely to occur, so try to ensure your breasts are emptied regularly. If you think you have blocked milk ducts, it's important to treat this early as it could otherwise develop into mastitis.

If your baby is not latching on properly, this can cause your milk ducts to become blocked, so check she is latching on correctly (see pages 18-23). Make sure, too, that your bra fits comfortably and not too tightly as this can cause problems too.

The best way to cure blocked ducts is by fully emptying your breasts, if necessary using a breast pump to help you (see page 34). What may also help is massaging your breast downwards using your fingers as your baby sucks.

If you are having difficulty getting rid of the blockages in your milk ducts and your breasts becomes hot and red or you develop a temperature, seek advice from your GP at once. This could be the start of mastitis, for which you may need medical treatment.

Mum's top tip

My advice is to check your breasts for blocked ducts, which can occur in the early weeks when your breasts become engorged with milk. Make sure they're fully drained by expressing any remaining milk at the end of a feed. Shift any blockages by massaging your breast downwards as your baby feeds. If the blockage is in an awkward spot – the underside of your breast, for instance – I found that feeding my baby in a different position really helped.

Mastitis

Mastitis can be a very painful condition that makes you feel unwell. It is basically an inflammation of the breast, which can become infected if it isn't dealt with promptly. It is caused by the breast not being adequately emptied of milk. The symptoms to watch out for are blocked milk ducts and red patches appearing on the breast. Often, the breast feels hot and painful and you may develop flu-like symptoms such as aching bones and a high temperature. The best course of action is to empty the breast of milk and to keep breastfeeding as this will help decrease the inflammation. If your baby is having trouble feeding from the infected breast, you should use a breast pump to empty it (see page 34) . If your symptoms show no sign of abating, you should see your GP at once as you may need a course of antibiotics.

Too much milk or fast flow

Sometimes your breasts may overproduce milk (normally at the beginning). Your body will eventually regulate the supply, but it can be uncomfortable in the meantime. If you are overproducing, try to express small amounts of milk in between feeds. You should find that, after a few days, your supply will become regulated and you won't be experiencing any further discomfort.

Another common problem is for the milk flow to be too fast for your baby. If she pulls away crying from your breast after a very short period of feeding, it could be due to this. One way of rectifying it is to use a nipple shield, which means the milk only comes into your baby's mouth when she sucks.

 For the **gurgle** video on **Milkbanking**, go to **gurgle.com** and click on **Videos**

Choosing to bottlefeed

Bottlefeeding: the lowdown

Ultimately it is up to you whether you choose breast or bottle for your baby. As long as you have weighed up the pros and cons of each method, you are entitled to make your own decision based on what suits you and your baby best.

If you have been advised not to breastfeed due to health reasons or because you are experiencing other difficulties, you may decide that you need to bottlefeed your baby.

Do try to remember that the first few weeks of breastfeeding (as you learn the new skill and adapt to it physically) are the hardest and, with a little help and support from your midwife, health visitor or breastfeeding counsellor, you will probably find that your problems disappear. It's well worth persevering if you can, so do seek guidance if you need to.

Formula milk has been rigorously designed to ensure that it supplies the best possible combination of vitamins and other nutrients. Several different brands are available, but although they each try to offer something different, the important thing to remember is that, fundamentally, and by law, they contain the same ingredients.

What to buy

If you are planning on bottlefeeding, you should make sure you have all the necessary equipment in advance of giving birth. It is wise to be prepared as that way you can familiarize yourself with the equipment and procedures involved.

A wide range of different shapes and kinds of bottle is available. Handle some to see which you find easiest to hold. Smaller bottles (120ml/4oz) and teats (with slow flow) for newborns will be necessary at first. As your baby gets a bit older, you can buy 225ml (8oz) bottles that hold more milk.

YOU WILL NEED
- Six bottles
- Six teats – make sure you get the right teat size for the age of your baby (i.e. newborn, 3–6 months, etc.)
- Sterilizing equipment: either a microwaveable sterilizer, a steamer or sterilizing solution to make up yourself. Follow instructions carefully as thorough sterilizing is vital to protect your baby from bacteria and bugs
- Muslin cloths to protect your clothing

 For the **gurgle** video on **Sterilizing your equipment**, go to **gurgle.com** and click on **Videos**

I'd say it's worth investing in a sterilizer even if you're planning to breastfeed. As well as bottles and teats, you can put breast pumps, dummies, dishes, cups and spoons in it. If you're planning to wash bottles by hand, I recommend washing them in hot, soapy water using a bottle brush, then sterilizing bottles and teats for ten minutes in a pan of boiling water on the hob.

Choosing to bottlefeed

Different teats

Teats come with different levels of flow (a variable-sized hole), depending on your baby's age and appetite. You may start your baby on a teat with a relatively small hole, but as he gets older and becomes hungrier, you may decide that it's time to progress to the next size up. For newborns, there's a level 0 teat which has a very slow flow so your baby isn't overwhelmed by the amount of milk coming out of the bottle; level 1 has a fairly slow flow; 2 is a bit faster and suited to a slightly older or hungrier baby; level 3 has a very fast flow. If you have any queries about whether your baby is ready to move to the next level, do ask your health visitor.

Choosing formula milk

Unless you have been otherwise advised by a doctor, cow's milk-based infant formula is the first choice of bottle 'food' for your baby. If your baby is allergic to cow's milk (see pages 162–7), goat's milk is sometimes recommended as an alternative as it contains similar proteins to that of cow's milk and is comprised of the same levels of lactose. But neither goat's nor sheep's milk contains sufficient nutrients, such as iron, unless they have been added. If you want to feed your baby these milks, then you must consult your GP first. Neither have been approved for use in Europe.

As with all baby-associated paraphernalia, a huge range of formula milk is available. It can be hard work choosing a brand as they all seem to promise different things and you want the best for your child. But panic not – they are all very similar. Indeed, it's worth bearing in mind that, by law, all formula milk basically contains the same ingredients. If you are concerned, however, then ask your health visitor or GP for advice as they probably have a favourite brand that they can recommend.

Tins of powdered milk are the cheapest option, although you will have more preparation to do than if you buy the more expensive cartons of ready-made formula. Powdered milk is available for different ages of infant, so choose the correct one for your baby's age. The carton milk doesn't have to be heated. It can be stored at room temperature before it is opened and kept afterwards in the fridge. If you are out and about quite a bit, then cartons are definitely more convenient. Maybe you could mix and match?

The right sort of milk

Don't forget: Formula milk is the only alternative to breast milk in the first six months of your baby's life and should be given for the first year. It is not safe to give babies ordinary full-fat milk (the type adults and older children drink) until they are a year old, although you may use it in cooking once your baby is six months old.

How much formula milk does my baby need?

All formula milk comes with instructions explaining how to make up the right amount for your baby. Formula milk is available for different ages of infant and you should make sure your baby is drinking the correct one for his age. Don't add extra milk powder into your baby's bottle as this will provide unnecessary calories and may encourage too many fat cells to be produced.

There is no precise answer to how much formula milk your baby should be having overall. When your baby is newborn, he will only take small feeds – probably around 60ml (2fl oz) at each meal. But this will of course increase rapidly as he grows. The amount of milk a baby needs is generally given as around 75–80ml ($2^1/_2$–$2^3/_4$fl oz) for each 0.5kg (1lb) of body weight. Therefore if your baby weighs 4kg (10lb), he would need about 750ml (25fl oz) of formula milk per 24-hour period.

As a rule, bottlefed babies feed less often than breastfeeding ones. This is due to the speed with which the different milks are digested, formula milk taking longer. On average, your baby will probably feed from the bottle about six times during a 24-hour period.

Bottlefed babies are rarely underfed, but it is important to feed on demand and not at the times you dictate. Check that the teat on the bottle is large enough for your baby's needs. If he cries and is upset – especially at the end of a feed, when the bottle is completely empty – then try offering him a little more milk.

When your baby hits six months and starts eating solids, the amount of milk he consumes will decrease, as he fills himself up with food other than milk. But if you have any concerns about your baby's development while bottlefeeding, do talk to your midwife or health visitor.

Feeding advice

It is more likely that you will try to give your baby more milk than if you were breastfeeding. For this reason, it's important to let him decide when he has had enough to drink so you don't overfeed him. While it's fine to give your baby more milk if he appears unsatisfied at the end of feed, it is bad practice to try and make him finish every last drop if he seems satisfied with what he has already drunk.

- Always follow the manufacturer's instructions when making up a formula feed to ensure your baby is receiving the right quantities of formula and water.

- Throw away the contents of any unused bottles of formula milk after 24 hours. (See advice overleaf.)

- Throw away ready-to-feed containers of formula milk after 48 hours once they have been opened.

- Throw away any formula milk left over after a feed as bacteria from your baby's saliva may contaminate it.

Bottlefeeding correctly

If you do decide to bottlefeed, it's important that you know how to do it correctly. Making up enough milk in advance for the day ahead is what many people used to do, although this may now change.

The UK Department of Health and the Food Standards Agency have recently changed their advice on the preparation and storage of powdered infant formula milk. They now advise you to make up a fresh bottle for each feed rather than preparing enough bottles of milk for the day. This is because of the small risk of salmonella bacteria developing in the (non-sterile) formula milk. While preparation of formula milk may take a little more time, this does cut down the risk of your baby being infected.

 For the **gurgle** video on **Bottlefeeding correctly**, go to **gurgle.com** and click on **Videos**

Mum's top tip

When travelling or away from home, I found ready-made formula so convenient! But you need to take great care when opening the carton to make sure you don't contaminate the liquid with any germs you may have on your fingers. I used to carry a pair of clean scissors with me to cut the corner off the carton then pour out the milk without touching the carton top at all.

Making up a feed

1 First of all, ensure that your hands are washed and the bottle you are using is both clean and sterile, then fill an empty kettle with cold water from the tap and boil it. Never use mineral water or old water that has been sitting around in the kettle.

2 Measure out the required amount of water – a temperature greater than 70°C (158°F) is required, which means water that has not been left for more than an hour to cool after boiling – and then add the milk powder to it. **Note:** All formula tins come with full instructions but generally one scoop of powder is added to 30ml (1fl oz) of water.

3 Put on the teat and lid and shake the bottle well to dissolve the powder. If not using immediately, place the bottle in the fridge for future use – bearing in mind the new government guidelines (see opposite and below). Don't use made-up milk that is over 24 hours old and throw away any milk left in the bottle after a feed.

4 The UK Department of Health and the Food Standards Agency recommend that if parents need to make up a feed for later, they keep freshly boiled water in a sealed flask and make up fresh formula when it is needed. The alternative to this would be using the ready-made cartons of formula milk.

Cartons of formula can be served straight from the cupboard at room temperature, or if your baby prefers, you can warm them up by standing the bottle in hot water or using a bottle warmer, as you would do for chilled made-up bottles of formula.

How to bottlefeed your baby

1 To prepare your baby for a feed, you should first make up the feed (see previous page), change your baby's nappy if it's dirty and choose a comfortable place to sit, preferably with your back well supported by cushions. Make sure you have a cloth to clean up any possetted milk and perhaps something to help occupy the time, such as a book, magazine or the radio.

2 Getting your baby in the right position for bottlefeeding is not as crucial as for breastfeeding (see pages 18–23) but she still needs to be in a good position for latching on to the teat so that she receives a good supply of milk. Hold your baby so her head is in the crook of your elbow and she's in a slightly raised position.

3 Test the temperature of the milk by pouring a little onto the back of your hand and then get your baby to 'root' (search) for the teat by stroking her cheek. She should open her mouth and you can put the teat inside.

4 Find a good angle for the bottle to be held and let your baby feed. If you want to change arms, insert a finger into the side of her mouth in order to gently release the teat. If you don't do this, you will be surprised by the strength of your baby's suction and may not be able to release the bottle!

5 Keep the bottle tilted to ensure that the teat is always filled with milk and doesn't contain any air. If your baby is regularly suffering from wind, you may want to experiment using slower-flowing teats or different shapes and styles of feeding bottle. Make sure that you feed your baby in an upright or near-upright position, as this will help any air bubbles to escape.

6 At the end of the feed, or possibly earlier if she seems uncomfortable and grumpy, you should wind your baby thoroughly so that she can fall asleep without being in any discomfort. Bottlefed babies tend to feed more quickly as a rule, and therefore tend to take in more air as they go.

7 If she suffers from a lot of wind, it might be worth changing the teat flow. A hole that allows the milk to come into her mouth too quickly is probably too large, allowing air to rush in as well, giving her wind.

8 If your baby seems dissatisfied with or exasperated by the amount of milk she is getting, she may not be receiving a fast enough flow. If this is the case, try making the teat hole larger by using a sterilized needle, or invest in some teats that allow a faster flow of milk.

Bottlefeeding correctly

Winding your baby

However you have chosen to feed your baby, whether you are bottlefeeding or breastfeeding, he will need to be winded. The best position for winding him is to have him sitting upright on your lap.

It's rather hard to get a baby to sit straight. A good way of doing it is to press one hand into the small of his back while you support him with your other hand, gently holding him under the chin. He can lean into your body side-on for extra support. This should do the trick.

Another position for winding your baby that is generally effective is to hold him over your shoulder (see the picture opposite), so he is facing the opposite direction to the way you are. The only disadvantage is that it can be a bit messy; there's a high chance of your shoulder being covered in baby milk! To protect your clothing it's a good idea to place a cloth over your shoulder. As long as your baby is not a champion projectile-vomiter, this should serve as a bib.

Usually, it won't take long for your baby to bring up wind, so you shouldn't have to wait too long before settling him down for a post-prandial sleep.

Whether you are breast- or bottlefeeding, your baby will probably take in small amounts of air along with his feed. This can then become trapped in his tummy and intestines, causing pain. Wind can prevent your baby from feeding properly, as he may feel full before he's had a proper feed; he may even bring up his feed together with any trapped air. There are several ways you can help prevent problems caused by wind, both during feeding and afterwards.

How to prevent wind while feeding

Breastfed babies tend to experience fewer problems with wind, as they can control the flow of milk better and go at their own pace, which means they take in less air. However, even breastfed babies can have problems with wind, especially if they are particularly fast feeders, or if you have fast-flowing milk.

As bottlefed babies tend to feed more quickly, they are likely to take in more air as they suck. Hold the bottle at an angle to ensure that the teat is always filled with milk and doesn't contain any air. If your baby is regularly suffering from wind, you may want to experiment with using slower-flowing teats or different shapes and styles of feeding bottle. (For advice on how to bottlefeed correctly, see pages 58–61.)

If your baby pauses for a break during a feed, you can use this opportunity to tilt him gently forwards against the palm of your hand while supporting his chin, and rubbing or gently patting his back to try and bring up any air. Don't try and force your baby to take a 'winding break' – this will probably just result in him starting to cry and therefore taking in more air.

Winding after a feed

Before you start winding after a feed, make sure that you have a muslin cloth handy, as many babies will bring up a certain amount of their feed along with the wind!

Try different winding techniques to see which best suits your baby, and remember that changing position from the one in which you have been feeding is usually the key. Placing your baby over your shoulder or across your lap and gently rubbing his back can be very effective for releasing any trapped wind. Alternatively, you may want to try simply sitting him up, leaning slightly against the palm of your hand while you support his chin, and gently rubbing his back with your other hand. A warm bath and gently massaging your baby's tummy in a circular motion can also work wonders.

If after a few minutes your baby hasn't brought up any air, don't keep trying to wind him. It may be that he doesn't have any to bring up, or he may release it later. Most babies stop having trouble with wind once they reach the stage of being able to change position on their own, and once their digestive tracts are more developed.

 For the **gurgle** video on **Winding your baby**, go to **gurgle.com** and click on **Videos**

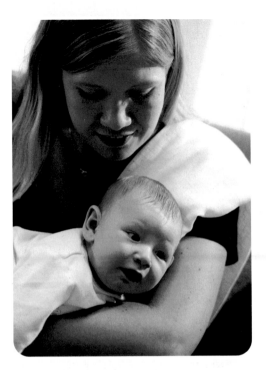

Using medication to treat wind

Herbal remedies can be helpful in easing wind in both babies and adults – dill, ginger, chamomile, fennel, catnip and lemon balm act in various different ways to soothe the gut and help break down any accumulated air. The traditional remedy gripe water contains several active herbal ingredients, although it is now alcohol-free. Ask your pharmacist for more information.

If your baby suffers badly from wind, your GP may suggest trying a commercially produced solution used for treating colic and which can be bought over the counter. This has to be given to your baby before each feed, and works by breaking down the air into smaller bubbles that are more easily expelled. It can be given to babies from birth onwards.

Bottlefeeding your premature baby

Having a premature baby – one that is born before 37 weeks of pregnancy – can be an emotional rollercoaster for the parents. Whether or not she needs to be looked after in a special care unit, one of the most crucial aspects of caring for her will be how to feed her. Even if you're planning on bottlefeeding, giving breast milk in the early days can provide your baby with vital nutrients.

A premature baby's stomach is smaller than a full term baby's, so her feeds need to be smaller yet more frequent (at least every three hours). Additionally, many premature babies don't have the strength to suck from either a teat or nipple in the beginning. Their intestines may also not be developed enough to properly absorb food. If this is the case with your premature baby and she is unable to feed from bottle or breast, here are some feeding options to consider.

INTRAVENOUS FEEDING
Very small or unwell babies may be unable to swallow or digest food for themselves. Instead, they will need to be fed special liquid meals via a fine tube directed into their veins. At some point, a baby may also be given the antibody-rich colostrum that her mother's body makes in the 72 hours after delivery (see pages 16–17). Once she can digest food, she can progress to naso-gastric feeding.

NASO-GASTRIC FEEDING
If your baby is able to digest food but unable to take it in through her mouth, she may be fed through a special fine tube passed through her nose into her stomach. She won't find this uncomfortable and, besides, being fed in this way will help her grow so that she can begin to feed normally.

When you notice your baby opening and shutting her mouth during her feeding times, you should encourage her sucking reflexes to develop by putting her into a good breastfeeding position so that she can nuzzle your breast. You may be able to express your breast milk which can then be given to your baby via the feeding tube.

COMBINATION FEEDING
Once your baby is a little older and more developed, it will be possible to start feeding her by mouth, even if this has to be topped up with tube-feeding. The baby's sucking and gag reflexes need to be developed enough to cope with oral feeding. When she is ready, you can try a combination of breast or bottle alongside tube-feeding. This combination feeding can continue until your baby is sufficiently developed to take just breast or bottle.

Your healthcare practitioner will advise you when the time is right for your baby. Once your baby has entirely stopped tube-feeding, she will progress to normal breast- or bottlefeeding.

Bottlefeeding a premature baby with breast milk

The nutrients in breast milk are invaluable to a newborn, even if you just provide her with the antibody-rich colostrum that your body makes in the 72 hours after delivery, and then afterwards switch to bottlefeeding. (For more on the benefits of breastfeeding a premature baby, see pages 36–9.)

It is possible to feed your baby breast milk via a naso-gastric tube initially. When she is ready and can coordinate breathing, sucking and swallowing, she can progress to a special feeding cup (from 32 weeks of age) or bottle, into which you can express your breast milk. It should be pointed out that some healthcare practitioners do not recommend using a cup, while others do.

Because of their immature digestive systems, breast milk is extremely good for premature babies, helping to protect against the rare but serious condition called necrotizing enterocolitis (NEC), where the intestines become damaged due to infection and a poor blood supply. NEC is more common in bottlefed premature babies. Breast milk also helps protect against allergies and infections, boosting a premature baby's immune system.

If you are going to express milk for your premature baby, you can either express by hand or use a specially-designed breast pump. Manually or electrically operated models are available. (For more on expressing breast milk, see pages 32–5.)

If your premature baby is having difficulty breastfeeding, she can be fed breast milk from a bottle. However, when she's more fully developed, she may then find it hard to get used to the different sucking style that breastfeeding requires. In which case, you may end up giving her formula milk from a bottle.

Bottlefeeding a premature baby with formula milk

It is possible to bottlefeed a premature baby with formula – once she can coordinate breathing, sucking and swallowing – although it may be recommended that you try giving her breast milk, at least in the short term. As we have seen, giving your premature baby breast milk equips her with vital nutrition from the start, which is particularly beneficial to a child who has been born early and needs all the extra help she can to catch up developmentally.

A specially-designed formula milk is available for premature babies. Your medical advisors are best placed to recommend the right formula for your baby's needs.

Your baby will probably need to be fed at least every couple of hours, but your midwives will advise you of the specific needs of your baby. One of the difficulties you may encounter in getting your baby to feed is constant sleepiness. She is likely to spend most of her time sleeping. Encouraging her to feed, as well as keeping her awake long enough to feed properly, can be hard work.

Equipment

You can start bottlefeeding your premature baby with a bottle and teat specially designed to fit her mouth. Using this special-sized equipment will encourage your baby to suck and swallow properly. She'll then have no trouble adapting to a normal-sized bottle and teat when she's a bit older.

Bottles for premature babies have a limited capacity of up to 50ml (1$\frac{3}{4}$fl oz). This is because your baby's stomach is so small she won't be able to tolerate much milk at any one time. But as long as your baby is wetting about 6–8 nappies a day, you can rest assured she is getting enough food.

Mum's top tip

Peta Hough, 31, experienced first hand the challenges of feeding her premature baby, Naomi, who was born at 35 and a half weeks. Naomi was jaundiced, extremely sleepy and needed to be woken up frequently to be fed, although she wasn't in a special care unit.

'I felt anxious about feeding her because I had to be so very vigilant about getting fluids into her at regular intervals. It was difficult because she was so sleepy and had to keep being woken up. I was taught to gently pinch her cheek and talk to her a lot in order to encourage her to wake.'

Milk-feeding routines and common problems

The right routine for your baby and you

Getting your child into a routine for feeding and sleep is the bane of most new parents' lives and tends to dominate new-mum discussions. There is no right or wrong when it comes to establishing a routine, but it is useful to introduce a structure into your baby's day so that he knows what is coming next and so that you can start to feel less disorganized and more in control.

Babies love routines and they're good for parents too. It's great to know that you'll be having a bit of 'you' time between 7 and 11pm, for example. If you try to do the same thing each night – bathtime, story, pyjamas, cuddle and bed – your baby will start to know what comes next and bedtime won't be a complete shock.

gurgle expert Sue Whytock, a nursery nurse for many years, maternity nurse and recently presenter of programmes such as *Help! I'm a Teenage Mum* and *Britain's Youngest Mums and Dads*, has provided gurgle with some tried and tested feeding routines for parents to follow (see overleaf).

The first is a routine suitable from three to ten weeks (you may want to focus on bonding with your baby in the first few weeks), while the second is from ten weeks onwards. The trick is to follow the routine but to stay reasonably flexible. It shouldn't take over your life or stop you leaving the house. In essence, it is to be taken with a pinch of salt! You will probably make your own adaptations to these routines, but they make a good starting point.

Talk with your GP or health visitor about any concerns you may have about your baby's feeding patterns or growth. Always make a point of raising any questions you may have when you go for your regular baby weigh-in sessions.

Milk-feeding routines and common problems

If at any stage you are worried that your baby is not putting on weight or growing, talk to your GP, who can run a series of checks to see if there are any other reasons stopping your child from thriving.

Feeding every three hours: three to ten weeks

7am Wash and change ready for food, then feed.

8am Playtime on mat.

8.30am Sleep back in cot or Moses basket.

10am Another feed.

11am Playtime or out for a walk.

1pm Feed.

2.30pm Sleep in cot.

3.45pm Wake up ready for feed.

4.00pm Feed – some babies will sleep after this feed and others will lose this nap and stay awake until their next one.

5.45–6pm Bathtime.

6.30–6.45pm Feed then bed. Feed him in his room – which may well be your bedroom for his first six months or so, keeping it semi-dark and quiet, and then settle your baby down for the night. When you leave the room, turn any nightlights off.

10.30–11.00pm Feed. Change your baby's nappy to wake him up so that he feeds well before going back to sleep.

3.00am Feed. Don't change your baby's nappy unless you have to as this will wake him up completely, whereas you want to keep him sleepy so he falls back to sleep.

Feeding every four hours: ten weeks onwards

7am Wash and change ready for first feed of the day. Feed.

8.45-9am Sleep.

10.00-10.45am Wake up from nap.

11.00am Feed.

12.45pm Sleep in cot.

2.45pm Wake up and change nappy.

3.00pm Feed and playtime.

5.45–6pm Bathtime.

6.30–6.45pm Feed. Always give a little more at this feed (although if you are breastfeeding, this may be difficult to judge). Feed in your baby's room and keep it semi-dark and quiet so that he settles for the night. When he has settled, leave the room and turn off any nightlights. If you can encourage your baby to fall asleep on his own (without being rocked or cuddled or fed to sleep), it will be better for you as once he learns to fall asleep on his own he will put himself back to sleep at night. For young babies this will take some time, however.

11pm Feed – first changing your baby's nappy to wake him up so he feeds well. Keep the room semi-dark and quiet so he goes back to sleep afterwards.

4.00-4.30am Feed. After about three and a half months, you can start thinking about encouraging your baby to sleep through the night.

Common problems

In the early days and weeks of your baby's life, you will be visiting your GP or health visitor regularly for baby weigh-ins and growth checks. Any concerns you have about your baby's growth, development or feeding patterns can be talked over at these appointments. Your concerns are important to your GP and health visitor, so consult them whenever you need information or reassurance about your baby's health and wellbeing.

Always check with your GP or health visitor if you are concerned about any aspect of your baby's wellbeing. No question is too trivial if you are anxious about something and need to know what to do about it. The following pages list some of the common problems that you may encounter and how to deal with them.

Vomiting

Vomiting is very common in babies and young children and can often happen when nothing is wrong. Your baby may 'posset' up her feed, bringing up a tiny amount of milk, usually after the feed or while being winded, and this is completely normal. If she brings up most or all of her feed, it is more likely that she is vomiting, but try not to panic. All babies are sick from time to time, whether they are breast- or bottlefed, and they usually get better within 24 hours.

WHEN TO CALL A DOCTOR
Call a doctor if your child continues to vomit over a six-hour period, has diarrhoea or a fever of over 38°C (100.4°F) or you notice other symptoms such as a rash, earache or dehydration (sunken eyes or fontanelle, dizziness or drowsiness).

CAUSES OF VOMITING

Your baby may be vomiting for a number of different reasons, usually very minor. The most common (and a few much rarer causes) are listed below.

- If your baby has drunk too much milk, it may cause her to vomit. She may just bring up the surplus milk, but sometimes the whole feed may come up. If this is the case she will probably only vomit once after the feed.

- Indigestion can cause your baby to vomit, so try not to rush her feeds.

- Occasionally babies can have an allergy to the proteins in their mother's breast milk and this may cause her to vomit. Consult your doctor if you suspect this is the case. You may be advised to change your diet or give your baby a hypoallergenic formula for a while. (For more on allergies, see pages 162–9.)

- Gastroenteritis or stomach flu, due to a viral or bacterial infection of the stomach and intestines, is a common cause of infant vomiting. Usually accompanied by diarrhoea, there may also be fever and a loss of appetite. If symptoms persist for more than six hours, consult your doctor.

- A fit of coughing can sometimes make your baby vomit, the force of the coughing causing her stomach to bring up her feed. If this is the case she will probably only vomit a few times, but if she keeps vomiting, get in touch with your doctor.

- Other illnesses that can be accompanied by vomiting include: urinary tract infections, ear infections, meningitis, appendicitis, pneumonia and Reye's syndrome.

- Reflux can also cause babies to vomit (see pages 84–5).

- An upset tummy due to something your baby has eaten can cause her to vomit, and will most likely be accompanied by diarrhoea, loss of appetite, general irritability and occasionally fever. This should not last for long, but if the symptoms do persist for more than six hours, then consult your doctor.

- Excessive crying may sometimes cause your baby to vomit as she takes in gulps of air.

- If your baby has a very runny nose and swallows a lot of mucus, it can cause her to vomit. Treat her symptoms as you would a common cold.

- If your baby has swallowed something toxic (such as a cleaning product or medicine), try to identify what she has swallowed and call 999.

WHAT TO DO IF YOUR CHILD IS VOMITING
If your child vomits for more then six hours, consult a doctor. If diarrhoea, fever, earache or a severe rash accompanies vomiting, seek medical help.

INFANTS UNDER SIX MONTHS
Offer your baby small but frequent amounts (about 2–3 teaspoonfuls) of oral electrolyte solution every 15–20 minutes. This contains salt and sugar and replaces important nutrients her body relies on but which it may have lost due to a bout of vomiting. Always read the instructions of the solution carefully

Milk-feeding routines and common problems

and give the right dose for the age of your baby. This will help to stop your child becoming dehydrated. (For more on dehydration, see pages 80–84.)

If your child goes for eight hours without vomiting, gradually re-introduce her normal formula feeds, offering her little and often to give her tummy the chance to get used to feeding again.

For breastfed infants, if the sickness seems to cease, breastfeed your child for five minutes every two hours. If, over an eight-hour period, she manages to keep her feed down, you can resume her normal routine.

INFANTS OF 6–12 MONTHS
As with infants under six months, offer your baby small but frequent amounts (about 2–3 teaspoonfuls) of oral electrolyte solution every 15-20 minutes to prevent her becoming dehydrated.

After eight hours of no vomiting, you can re-introduce formula feeds slowly, not giving your child too much at a time. Offer feeds of 30–60ml (1–2 fl oz), gradually working up to the normal feeding routine .

For breastfed infants, follow the advice given for babies of under six months.

After eight hours, you can try to give your baby small amounts of bland foods such as bananas or mild baby food.

FOR CHILDREN OVER 12 MONTHS
Give clear liquids such as water, but dilute fruit juice and avoid giving milk.

As with younger babies, give your child oral electrolyte solution to help replace lost salt and sugars, carefully following the instructions on the packet. If your child vomits up the solution, start again with small teaspoonfuls.

After eight hours of no vomiting, try giving your child bland, soft, easy foods such as soup, toast (with no butter) and banana. If after 24 hours your child is no longer vomiting, she can resume her normal diet.

Pyloric stenosis

Pyloric stenosis is a rare condition that affects babies in the first few months of life. It occurs because the muscle controlling the valve that leads from the stomach to the intestines thickens so much that food is unable to pass through.

SYMPTOMS
Your baby will start to projectile vomit and will be unable to keep any food down.

TREATMENT
If this is the case, consult your doctor immediately as your baby may need an operation to rectify the problem and unblock the valve.

Dehydration

Babies and children can suffer from dehydration because they are more prone to diarrhoea and vomiting due to childhood illnesses and picking up infections at nursery or school. We all need to drink a healthy supply of water to maintain our body chemistry and to carry waste products out of our bodies. If your child loses water due to vomiting, diarrhoea or fever and does not replace the water he has lost, it may result in dehydration.

HOW SERIOUS IS DEHYDRATION?
Dehydration is very serious as it can lead to brain damage and even death so should be considered as an emergency. Even mild dehydration means your child will have lost essential nutrients and his blood volume could fall dangerously low.

WHAT ARE THE SYMPTOMS OF DEHYDRATION?

If your baby has a dry mouth and lips, as well as being very drowsy and hard to rouse, he may be suffering from dehydration. If he is under 18 months, check that the fontanelle (the soft patch at the very top of his head) is not sunken. If it is, this may indicate dehydration.

Keep an eye on his nappies. If you notice that his urine is a dark yellow or that his nappies are dry, he is probably dehydrated.

Here's a summary of symptoms to look out for:

● Dry nappies for more than four to eight hours
● No tears while crying
● A dry, parched mouth
● Lethargy
● Darker urine in his nappy

Signs of serious dehydration to look out for:

● Unresponsive behaviour
● Delirium or floppiness
● Sunken eyes
● Hands that feel cold and look blotchy
● Sunken fontanelle (if your baby is under 18 months)

HOW SHOULD I TREAT DEHYDRATION?

Reduce any fever your baby may have with infant paracetamol or dab his forehead with a tepid, damp sponge. If he is still bottlefed, replace his milk feeds with cooled, boiled water, either in his bottle or from a spoon or cup. Try giving him just water for six hours instead of milk. If you are breastfeeding, continue exclusively breastfeeding your baby as he should be getting enough fluid from the breast milk he drinks to rehydrate him. A doctor should be consulted if your baby continues to have diarrhoea, vomiting or fever for more than six hours or doesn't seem to get any better after you have given nothing except cooled, boiled water over this time.

For an older child, encourage him to drink something (preferably water) every ten minutes for a few hours. Avoid milk or fruit juice. If he is vomiting, it may be difficult for him to keep the fluid down, but you can rest assured that his body will be absorbing some fluid and it's certainly better than none at all. Try giving your child sips of water from a spoon so he is taking in small amounts all the time. The key here is to offer liquid little and often.

If he can keep any food down, try something like scrambled egg and plain bread. The egg will help to 'bind' him if he has diarrhoea.

Try an oral electrolyte solution, available from any chemist, to replace lost salts and glucose in your child's body. Remember to follow the instructions given on the packet, making sure the dosage is suitable for the age of your child. The solution should be given to him the moment it is made up. Please note too that it is best to check with your doctor first before you begin any treatment for dehydration.

HOW CAN I KEEP MY CHILD'S FLUID INTAKE UP?
If you are bottlefeeding, wait for the illness to pass, then dilute your baby's normal formula with three times the usual amount of cooled, boiled water. The water can gradually be reduced and replaced with the usual proportions of formula/water. For an older child, encourage him to drink water with his meals and, if he's thirsty, throughout the day.

Mum's top tip

I was surprised how quickly my baby became dehydrated in hot weather. When out and about in the summer months, I always carry a bottle of cooled, boiled water with me, to prevent my baby getting too thirsty. You'll know your baby's getting enough water if his nappies are wet and his urine pale. Darker urine is a sign of dehydration.

WHEN SHOULD I CALL A DOCTOR?

If you suspect your child is mildly dehydrated, make an appointment with your GP as soon as possible and keep administering fluids. If you suspect your child is seriously dehydrated, take him straight to your nearest casualty department, where he will probably be given fluids intravenously until his blood fluid levels return to normal.

Reflux in babies

Acid reflux, or gastro-oesophageal reflux disease (GORD), is a condition that can affect perfectly healthy babies in the first three months of life. At the base of the oesophagus – the tube that carries food from the mouth to the stomach – is a valve, a ringlike muscle called a sphincter, that lets food pass down to the stomach while stopping food or acid coming back up. In young babies whose digestive system in still immature, this valve is sometimes not developed enough to stop food from flowing back up through the oesophagus and into the mouth. This is what is known as reflux. The condition is also prevalent in premature babies whose stomachs haven't matured enough by the time they are born.

By the time your baby reaches 12–24 months, the sphincter has usually developed enough to stop the food from flowing the wrong way, and any reflux will have gone by then, if not sooner.

SYMPTOMS

If your baby brings up tiny amounts of milk after feeding, this is simply possetting and is completely normal. But if she is constantly bringing up milk it may be a sign of reflux. Other symptoms to look out for are:

- Your baby frequently vomiting up part or all of her feed
- Arching her back during a feed (because of the acidic pain, similar to heartburn, caused by reflux) or refusing to feed
- Crying excessively after feeding
- Constant hiccuping or coughing

- Waking frequently but calming down when she is upright – reflux tending to be worse when your baby is lying down. (Taken on its own, this may not be a symptom of reflux as babies frequently have disrupted sleep during the first few months of their lives and are calmed when picked up)
- Poor weight gain
- Blood in your baby's stools.

DIAGNOSIS AND TREATMENT

Your doctor will examine your baby while you describe her symptoms. If he can't make an immediate diagnosis, she may need to be referred for further tests. This might involve passing a fine tube down her throat to measure the levels of acid in the oesophagus, or looking at her stomach via an endoscope (a flexible instrument with a tiny camera at one end).

In most cases, your doctor will be able to diagnose your baby on the spot and she won't need further testing. As long as she is healthy, contented and feeding well, she is unlikely to need any treatment as the reflux will probably go away by itself.

If your baby is bottlefed, your doctor may suggest that you thicken up her formula with a special powder as well as keeping her more upright while feeding. If she's breastfed, it is possible to give a small amount of the powder made up with cooled, boiled water before and after she feeds. It might also be a good idea to give your baby smaller feeds to help her stomach cope with the flow of food until the sphincter at the end of her oesophagus has properly matured.

If your baby is having problems feeding and isn't gaining weight fast enough, she may need to be prescribed medicine to help keep the acid from coming back up. If the condition doesn't get better with medication, she may need further tests. Likewise if she becomes anaemic, has blood in her vomit, frequent chest infections or difficulty swallowing, she may need to see a specialist.

WEANING A BABY WITH REFLUX

Studies conducted on babies who suffer from reflux show that once they start solids they should avoid acidic drinks and acidic fruit and vegetables such as citrus fruit and tomatoes.

If your baby has reflux, there is no right or wrong time to wean her onto solids, especially if you feel that solid foods may help to keep her all-important milk feeds down. Whether you start to wean her at four months or closer to six will be up to you. If you decide to start at four months, you should take the process very slowly to let your baby's stomach get used to more complex foods. It's important to discuss your baby's nutritional needs with your doctor first before you start weaning.

FIRST FOODS FOR A BABY WITH REFLUX

Most babies are weaned on fruit and vegetables as their first foods, but babies with reflux can find some fruit and vegetables too acidic. You should avoid giving her pineapple, oranges, grapefruit, lemons, limes or tomato-based foods. Stick to green vegetables such as broccoli or cabbage and try using pumpkin, potato, cauliflower and parsnips in your baby's diet. If your baby has reflux, getting milk to stay down is very important because this is still her chief form of nutrition. The first weaning foods are really just to introduce her to taste and texture rather than to sustain her. Having said that, some parents find that solid food can help to keep the milk feeds down, making it a great help for a baby with reflux. But each baby is different, of course, responding to food differently, so some experimentation may be needed.

Some parents have found that a small amount of olive oil added to their baby's food can help with reflux because the oil binds to the bile acids (secreted into the intestines and assisting with digestion). But always talk to your doctor first if you are planning a new treatment for your baby, even if it's a natural method like this one.

Mum's top tip

Gastro-oesophageal reflux disease, commonly known as reflux, is defined as the pushing of food in the stomach back up into the oesophagus. It often emerges through the mouth, or even the nose. It usually occurs because the digestive system is underdeveloped. Reflux can be a real nightmare – and I should know. My five-year-old daughter, Olivia, spent the first two and a half years of her life not only vomiting up practically every meal, but also unable to chew properly. It really got me down – it's a mum's natural instinct to nurture her child, and I felt I was failing miserably. While my friends' children would happily eat a whole apple or chew a plate of chopped-up chicken and veg, I would have to laboriously purée everything Olivia consumed. This tiresome process continued until she was nearly three. If I did try to give her something even the slightest bit 'lumpy', she would either gag and then vomit, or store it in her cheeks like a hamster. This was incredibly disheartening and I would often find myself jealous of other mothers, who seemed to have it so easy. Furthermore, no one took my concerns seriously as my daughter was a healthy weight and always full of energy. I was treated like a neurotic, paranoid mum. Doctors were slow to diagnose her problem and I was even made to feel like I was to blame.

Eventually, I'd had enough – I knew something wasn't right with Olivia's feeding. Several months after her second birthday, she was tested for reflux and, sure enough, the results were positive. I was recommended a specific over-the-counter medicine, but luckily Olivia's condition began to improve and I didn't have to resort to treating her. I think going to nursery really helped, as she could mimic the other children's feeding habits. I just wish that she'd been diagnosed with reflux when she was a baby, so that I could have done something constructive sooner and spared us both all that heartache.

According to a nutritionist and trained breastfeeding counsellor, reflux is often over-diagnosed; she said that it's natural for babies to posset and it's not uncommon for them to have a loose sphincter. If children do have reflux, one reassuring statistic is that over 90% of them will grow out of it.

DIFFERENT TREATMENTS FOR REFLUX

When reflux is mild, it's often enough to keep your child upright. Sodium alginate, available from any chemist, can also help. This is mixed with the feed or dissolved in water after each meal. It works by forming a gel in the stomach and so preventing food from going back into the oesophagus. If your baby has reflux, it might be better to breastfeed rather than give formula milk. This is because breastfeeding helps to reduce acid in your baby's stomach which in turn can make reflux worse. Many women stop breastfeeding as they believe this will help, whereas the reverse is true: breastfeeding can actually help to combat the symptoms.

Other treatments for reflux include thickening milk or formula and keeping your child upright after a feed. There is varying evidence that keeping your baby at an angle while sleeping so that she isn't flat can help (using a special, wedge-shaped pillow), as can letting her nap in a bouncy chair during the day so that she remains more upright. If you do want to try any of these methods, always discuss them first with your GP.

It can help to slow down your baby's feed, or change infant formulas to see if this is what is making it worse. (Only change your baby's formula after consulting your doctor first.) In older children it is known that certain foods make reflux worse, including acidic fruit and vegetables (see above), full-fat milk, chocolate milk, sausage, bacon and fatty meat.

If reflux is more severe, medication can be prescribed. This helps to do one of two things: either to reduce the acid in the stomach or to improve the function of the digestive system. Less commonly, surgery may be performed – a portion of the stomach being wrapped round the oesophagus to create a valve at the top of the stomach. Surgery is obviously only to be considered as a last resort.

If your baby does have reflux, it can be quite upsetting for you as a parent, but be reassured that most children will grow out of it and your baby will soon be able to chomp away with the best of them!

Constipation

Breastfed babies rarely get constipated because breast milk is easy to digest and stools are softer, making bowel movements trouble-free. Bottlefed babies are more inclined to suffer from constipation because formula milk is less easy to digest and bowel movements will be thicker and fewer, making constipation more likely.

BABIES FROM BIRTH TO SIX MONTHS

It is perfectly normal for a small baby to have a bowel movement only a couple of times a day or even every few days. If you notice your baby hasn't had a bowel movement for a while and seems troubled by it (irritable, suffering from tummy cramps, wind and pulling his legs up to his tummy, or with blood in his nappies), consult your GP immediately. It is rarely serious but your GP can prescribe medicine specifically for a small baby when conventional medicine may be dangerous.

BABIES AGED FOUR TO SIX MONTHS

Somewhere around four to six months, your baby will start to be introduced to solids. This can cause slight constipation as his system gets used to new, more solid foods. The consistency and frequency of his bowel movements depend on what he eats, so if he is not getting enough fresh fruit, vegetables or liquids, he will be more prone to constipation. On the other hand, babies of this age may have a bowel movement several times day or just one every two to three days. You'll know what is 'normal' for your baby.

WHEN SHOULD I WORRY?

You should only be concerned if your child has gone longer than about four to five days without having a bowel movement (and is older than six months) and if he seems to be in pain, uncomfortable or has tummy cramps. You may also notice that his stools are hard and pebble-like, or that there is some blood in his nappy. If he is an older child, he may complain that he finds it hard to have a bowel movement or seems to be straining on the potty or loo. If you notice any of these symptoms, consult your doctor, who can prescribe a special laxative suitable for your child's age. Never give your child a laxative unless it has been prescribed, as general over-the-counter medication can be unsuitable for young children.

If your child has occasional bouts of constipation, there is nothing to worry about; it is probably his system getting used to new foods. If he has frequent or chronic constipation, you should make an appointment with your GP to rule out anything more serious.

HOW CAN I STOP MY CHILD GETTING CONSTIPATED?

- If he is on solids, encourage him to eat more fibre, giving him plenty of wholegrains (wholewheat bread, brown rice and cereals), fresh fruit and vegetables. Avoid giving him processed foods.

- Make sure your child gets lots of fluids, preferably water.

- Don't leave him sitting on the loo for a long time, especially when potty training, as this could discourage him from going. If he had an uncomfortable stool previously, he may be afraid of having another one and therefore hold it in, making things worse. A child may also hold in a stool as a way of resisting parents too eager to potty train him.

- Make sure you leave plenty of time for your child to have a bowel movement so it's not rushed. This is especially the case if you're out and about – on a shopping trip, for instance, or visiting a friend – as he may be reluctant to have a bowel movement when he's away from home.

HOW CAN I TREAT CONSTIPATION?
For a young baby:
- Massage your baby's tummy in an anti-clockwise motion
- Cycle his legs in the air for a short while
- Try giving him a warm bath as this can sometimes help
- If he is over six months, give him cooled, boiled water.

For an older child:
- Stewed prunes and dates can aid the regularity of bowel movements
- Give your child plenty of fluids
- Try to make sure he has a diet with enough fibre, including wholegrains, fresh fruit and vegetables
- Your doctor can prescribe special laxatives if necessary – never give your child a laxative that has not been prescribed If he is prescribed one, follow the instructions on the packaging very carefully to give the right dose for his age.

cook's tip Fruity Porridge – a great way of getting fruit into your little one's diet! Place 1 apple and 1 pear (each peeled, cored and chopped) and 4 dried apricots in a saucepan. Cover and cook until tender (about 6 minutes). In a separate pan, bring 15g ($\frac{1}{2}$oz) of porridge, 150ml (5fl oz) of milk and 4 tablespoons of water to the boil and simmer for 3 minutes. Combine the fruit and porridge, stirring well. Cool before serving.

Understanding your baby's stools

New parents are often fascinated by their baby's stools, spending ages contemplating their consistency and frequency and what these indicate about their baby's wellbeing. So how much can you tell from your baby's stools, and what should you be looking out for?

EARLY STOOLS

The stools of breast- and bottlefed babies look very different. Generally speaking, those of breastfed babies hardly smell at all, are mustard-yellow in colour and grainy in consistency. Those of bottlefed babies are usually yellow too, but are more bulky and tend to be smellier.

Frequency of bowel movements in babies can vary enormously. Some babies have several movements a day, while others have only one every few days. The two things to watch out for are constipation and diarrhoea.

OLDER BABIES AND TODDLERS

As your baby moves on to solid food, his stools will become bulkier and more unpleasant-smelling. To begin with, he may not be able to digest high-fibre foods, such as raisins, and these may pass through the gut and emerge in his stools virtually intact. The colour of the food he's eating will also affect the colour of his stools – tomato sauce may produce red stools, for instance, and puréed carrots ones that are more orange.

Children who are eating a varied and balanced diet that includes plenty of fresh fruit and vegetables, and are drinking enough fluids, should not suffer from constipation. But if you do suspect something is not quite right with your child, usually time-honoured remedies such as stewed prunes or figs will be enough to get things moving again.

Diarrhoea

Diarrhoea is when there is an abnormal increase in the frequency or liquidity of your baby or child's stools. Although not dangerous in itself, it can indicate more serious problems. The main thing to watch out for is dehydration as the food your child eats will be passing too quickly through her intestines for her to retain any of the water contained in it.

Frequent and watery stools result from irritation of the gut. It can be caused by a number of things, and it may clear up as soon as it started with no indication of the cause. Diarrhoea in young babies can be very serious, as they can become dehydrated extremely quickly as a result – a sunken fontanelle, the soft patch at the top of your baby's head, will indicate this. Be sure to give your baby sufficient water to reduce the risk of dehydration. (For more on this, including other symptoms of dehydration, see pages 80–84.)

DIARRHOEA IN BABIES

Bear in mind that babies on a milk diet, especially those who are breastfed, will have frequent and runny bowel movements, so these are nothing to worry about. A newborn baby who is breastfed can have roughly five bowel movements a day. She cannot store milk for very long in her tiny tummy, so you may notice her having a bowel movement with or after each feed. By the time she's a month old, she'll probably start to have fewer bowel movements. Bottlefed babies generally have fewer bowel movements and their stools are less runny. When your baby starts to eat solids, her stools will become firmer and less frequent. Loose, frequent stools at this age could signal diarrhoea. She might be reacting to something she has eaten or be suffering from gastroenteritis, especially if accompanied by fever or vomiting.

WHEN SHOULD I WORRY?

If your baby has no symptoms except for looser stools and seems happy enough, she may have eaten too much of one kind of food, especially one high in fibre, such as fruit. This kind of diarrhoea will probably clear up quickly by itself. However, you should call your doctor:

- If your baby is under 12 months and has had diarrhoea for more than six hours, especially if she has a fever and is in danger of becoming dehydrated

- If she has diarrhoea and abdominal pain around her navel and lower right side of her groin, as she may have appendicitis, which will require immediate hospitalization

- If your baby has abdominal cramps and is vomiting, and her bowel movements contain jelly-like mucus streaked with blood, as she may have a bowel blockage

- If her stools contain pus or streaks of blood, as this may indicate an intestinal infection or anal fissures

- If your child soils her underpants involuntarily but is otherwise potty-trained, as she may have a condition known as encopresis (with various causes)

- If your child has pale stools that are bulky and smelly and that float when you try to flush them away, as she may have coeliac disease (a hypersensitivity to gluten).

HOW TO TREAT DIARRHOEA

If your baby is breastfed, carry on feeding her as normal, keeping a close eye on the frequency of her bowel movements. If she is bottlefed, stop the milk feeds and give her cooled, boiled water from a bottle, cup or spoon. In either case, if the symptoms have not cleared up after six hours, consult your doctor. For older children, avoid giving any more food or milk and stick to frequent drinks of rehydration solution and water.

HOW TO AVOID DIARRHOEA

Encourage your child to wash her hands after she has been to the loo and also before eating so that germs and bacteria are not spread. Wash your hands after you have changed a nappy and before you prepare food, to help prevent the spread of germs.

Tongue tie

Tongue tie is a birth defect that occurs when the lingual frenulum
(the cord which attaches the tongue to the floor of the mouth) is
shorter, tighter and more restrictive than normal. This can impair
your baby's ability to breastfeed and, in some cases, causes speech
problems as he grows. Tongue tie tends to be an inherited condition
but can also happen out of the blue. It also tends to affect more
boys than it does girls.

DIAGNOSING TONGUE TIE

It can be hard to diagnose tongue tie as it is not easily
identifiable at first, often only coming to light because a
mother is having problem breastfeeding.

HOW TO CHECK FOR TONGUE TIE

- Your baby may have difficulty sticking out his tongue. Most
  babies can poke their tongues over their gums. Try playing a
  few tongue-poking games to see if your baby copies you.

- You may notice the frenulum or cord that attaches his tongue
  to the floor of his mouth is attached very close to the tip of
  his tongue. This may mean his tongue cannot move around as
  freely or loosely as it should.

- He may have trouble moving his tongue from side to side, so
  try a few games where you stick your tongue to one side of
  your mouth, then the other, to see if he can copy with ease.

- Can he cup his tongue well? If you place a finger into your
  baby's mouth, his tongue should wrap around it. Babies with
  tongue tie are often unable to do this.

- If your baby has a heart-shaped tongue (with a little 'V' in the
  centre of the tip of the tongue), he could have tongue tie as
  there appears to be a link between the two.

- If your baby is having difficulty latching on properly, this is
  one of the more obvious signs that your baby is tongue-tied.

DIFFICULTY FEEDING A BABY WITH TONGUE TIE

The tongue plays a major role in breastfeeding by helping to pull the nipple into position, catch milk before swallowing and create the right amount of suction. Babies with tongue tie cannot move their tongues as freely and so find it difficult to latch on; they may dribble excessively or need very long feeds because they can't empty the breast as efficiently. As a result, they may not be getting enough milk and therefore not gain weight as rapidly as they should.

In a study conducted by consultant paediatric surgeon Mervyn Griffiths, it was found that out of 215 babies under the age of three months, 88% had problems latching on before the division of the tongue. In addition, 77% of mothers had problems such as painful nipples. Do remember, though, that these problems are very common and don't automatically indicate tongue tie. You may just need a bit of help with breastfeeding (see pages 18–23 for advice).

COMMON FEEDING PROBLEMS FOR YOUR BABY

- He doesn't seem to be gaining enough weight even though you are breastfeeding.

- He seems to have difficulty latching on and you can hear him sucking in air as he feeds.

- He frequently stops and starts feeding (he can't create a good suction on the breast so keeps coming off).

My baby is seven months old and weighs only 14lb but he was premature. My doctor told me not get too worried about what his growth chart showed but instead to look at him and if he seemed happy and healthy, and was producing wet and dirty nappies, then to be reassured, because every baby is different and grows at his or her own pace.

- You notice him biting or chewing your breast (he is compensating by using his jaw to help with feeding).

COMMON PROBLEMS FOR YOU
- You feel pain in your breast towards the end of the feed (some babies with tongue tie cannot latch on properly at the end of the feed when they become tired and the milk flow is not as fast at the beginning).

- Your nipple is painful or squashed after a feed (resembling the end of a lipstick once it's been used).

Bear in mind that these are also common breastfeeding niggles and your baby may not be latching on for a different reason entirely. If you are worried, talk to your health visitor, who can help you find a lactation consultant in your area to give you advice on how to breastfeed your baby properly. Try not to lose heart or give up with breastfeeding. Lots of tongue-tied babies manage to breastfeed correctly and it may mean you both need a little help learning a new technique.

TREATMENT
Babies rarely need treatment for tongue tie as they tend to adapt and, in any case, the frenulum becomes looser during the first year. If your baby is tongue-tied but feeding well and gaining weight, there is no need for immediate treatment; he will be checked again at a later date. If breastfeeding and weight gain are a problem, simple surgery may be an option.

The most common treatment for tongue tie is a frenotomy, which involves the frenulum being snipped with sterile scissors while your baby is under a local anaesthetic. Luckily this is a very low-risk procedure that should not hurt your baby and cause very little loss of blood. Mothers are usually advised to start breastfeeding again as soon as possible after the procedure, although it may take your baby a little while to get used to his free-moving tongue. You may need some help from a lactation consultant to get breastfeeding back on the go again, so talk to your GP or health visitor, who can put you in touch with someone locally.

Failure to thrive

Some children do not gain weight or grow as much as they should. Although this can happen for a variety of reasons, it is usually just described as a failure to thrive.

REASONS FOR YOUR CHILD FAILING TO THRIVE
- If she is not getting enough food, or is not taking enough food in.
- She had a low weight at birth.
- She has had frequent childhood illnesses that have stopped her from taking food in, and hindered her growth.
- She has a disease that is hindering her growth such as kidney failure, malaria or TB.
- Some children suffering from emotional deprivation can fail to put on weight and grow properly.

FEEDING
Sometimes feeding techniques may be responsible for a baby's failure to thrive. If your baby doesn't latch on properly to the breast, she may fail to grow and put on weight. If she is very underweight or doesn't seem to be steadily putting on weight, talk to your doctor or health visitor, who can check that your baby is receiving milk properly from you. (If you think the problem may be because you're not breastfeeding correctly, see pages 18–23.)

Formula milk is a good alternative to breast milk if breastfeeding does not work for you. Babies who fail to gain weight while bottlefeeding may not be getting enough milk. Check that the teat is letting the right amount of milk through to your baby for her age, and check you are diluting formula and water to the recommended quantity. (Check the manufacturer's instructions as the amount can vary. See also pages 58–61 for advice on bottlefeeding correctly.)

If you are worried that your baby is not putting on weight or growing, talk to your GP who can run a series of checks to see if there are any underlying issues that may be preventing your child from thriving.

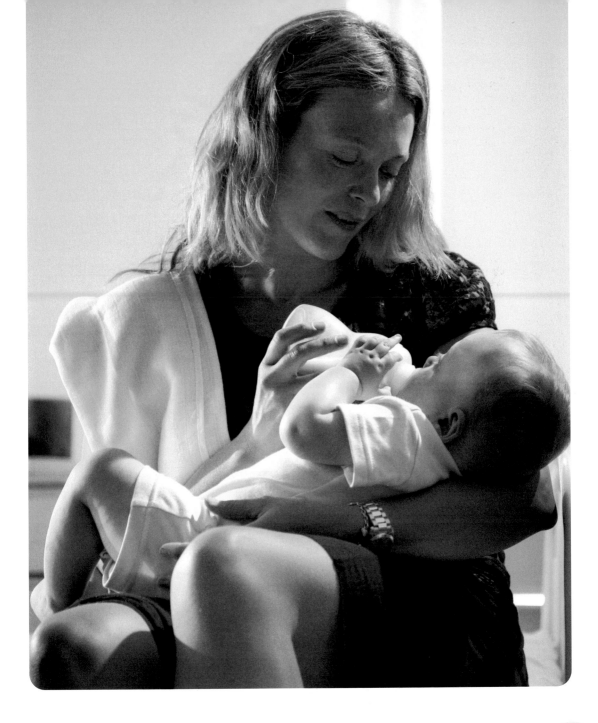

Starting solids

When is it safe to feed my baby solid food?

Breast milk or formula will provide all the nutrients a growing baby needs for at least the first four months of her life. In the UK, the Department of Health now recommends exclusive breast- or bottlefeeding for the first six months. It is thought that your baby's digestive system is unlikely to be sufficiently developed to cope with solids before then.

Up until recently, the advice was to try weaning your baby between four and six months of age, and waiting for six months may seem a little strict to mums with children brought up before the new advice was issued. Your baby's weight plays a big part, though. As a general rule, when she is roughly double her birth weight (usually at around six months but it can be a little before this), you will start to notice the signs that she is ready for solid foods.

Equally, it is inadvisable to leave weaning onto solids for longer than six months. One of the reasons for this is that the iron stores your baby inherited from you during pregnancy will have been used up and she will now need to absorb iron from food. (For more on the importance of iron in your baby's diet, see pages 116–19.)

There are a few simple indicators that your baby might be ready for weaning. For example, if she doesn't appear to be satisfied by her milk feeds, perhaps waking in the night when she didn't used to, this can indicate that she is ready to move on. Another sign that she is ready for solids is if she is showing interest in your food, reaching out for what's on your plate, or trying to put her hands in your mouth while you eat.

When is it safe to feed my baby solid food?　　

105

When is it safe to feed my baby solid food? 105

What to feed when

PRIOR TO SIX MONTHS
Whether breastfeeding or otherwise, you'll need to be aware that certain foods can cause an allergic reaction in babies and therefore should not be given before the age of six months, after which the immune system is better established (see page 112; for more on allergies, see pages 162–9).

FOODS TO TRY AFTER SIX MONTHS
- Cereals such as baby rice, millet and maize (all gluten-free).
- Puréed fruit and vegetables. Try sweet potato, avocado, carrot, swede, butternut squash, apple, pear or banana.

FROM SEVEN TO NINE MONTHS
- Cereals such as the gluten-free ones above.
- Wheat-based products (introduced slowly), such as cooked pasta shapes, and porridge.
- Leafy green vegetables as well as other fruit and vegetables.
- Puréed lentils.
- Mashed potato.
- Puréed meat (lean red meat or poultry) mixed with vegetables.
- Puréed fish mixed with vegetables (watching out for bones!).

FROM NINE TO 12 MONTHS
Up until this age, your baby is likely to be having only one meal a day consisting of solids. From nine months, she will be developing a real appetite for solid food and it's likely that you will have progressed to two or more meals a day. Probably, your baby will be eating breakfast, lunch and dinner. She will enjoy holding her food in her hands and will particularly delight in making a great mess everywhere. She'll also have teeth to help with the foods that are less puréed. In addition to all the other delicious foods you have been experimenting with, you can add a few new items:

- Well-cooked eggs
- Finger food, such as baby rice cakes and breadsticks
- Bread
- Fromage frais
- Yoghurt
- Oranges
- Strawberries and kiwi fruit (although monitor these carefully as some babies may be allergic to them).

Weaning a premature baby

The guidelines on when to wean a premature baby are somewhat unclear, so you should consult your GP or health visitor. In very general terms, the earlier your baby was born, the later weaning is recommended – usually some time between six and nine months. If your baby was born 12 weeks ago, for instance, but was four weeks early, her 'corrected' age is actually eight weeks rather than 12. You'll need to bear this in mind when you are thinking about weaning.

Because your baby's gut will take longer to mature, it's important not to wean her too early, as this could have a detrimental effect on her health. It's therefore vital that you discuss your baby's needs with your healthcare providers before you start weaning.

Generally speaking, it is recommended that full-term babies shouldn't be weaned until at least the age of four months (some practitioners say you shouldn't wean before a year) as the gut is not mature enough to cope with solid food. With this in mind, you should under no circumstances try to wean your premature baby before four months. By around the age of six months, milk alone is usually not sufficient for most babies' needs – whether or not they are premature. Your baby will probably give you signs that she is ready to wean (for example, a loss of interest in or complete refusal to breastfeed). If she has had stomach surgery or there is a family history of allergies, seek medical advice before weaning.

Should I feed my baby organic food?

When deciding what to feed your baby, it's easy to get confused by the mass of information and conflicting messages about organic food, most of which debate whether it's actually better for you. With most of us living in towns with limited space for growing vegetables, is it best to go for the most 'natural' option for your baby and choose organic? Despite the extra cost involved, it seems that buying organic could be worth it in the long run. Here are some reasons why.

- Your baby's body is much more vulnerable to pesticides because her kidneys and digestive system are immature and so not as proficient at excreting harmful substances.

- Greenpeace estimates that your body may contain up to 200 synthetic chemicals. Whatever harmful effects these have on an adult will be worse for a baby.

- Pound for pound, pre-school children eat on average 2–4 times more fruit and vegetables than adults and so are exposed to a higher proportion of possible contaminants.

- The health effects of chronic low-level exposure to pesticide residues, on adults and children, are still unknown.

- A report, *Pesticides in Children's Food*, by the Environmental Working Group, concludes that the largest contribution to a person's lifetime risk of cancer from pesticide residues occurs during childhood.

- Existing regulations on the amount of pesticide residues that non-organic baby foods may contain are based on 'acceptable' levels for adult consumption.

- Organic baby foods are produced without pesticides, antibiotics or growth hormones.

- No one yet knows what effect genetic modification may have on food products and the health of those who consume genetically modified food. Baby food that is organic is produced without genetically modified ingredients.

- Not only is it more nutritious in many instances (see below), but in a recent UK poll more than 70% of consumers reported that organic meat, fruit and vegetables taste better.

Is organic food really more nutritious?

It's tempting to think it's a no-brainer to buy organic food. But is there any evidence to suggest that organic food is more nutritious than non-organic? Well, actually, yes. An EU-funded project known as Quality Low Input Food – aiming to improve the quality and reduce the cost of organic and other 'low-input' food – found that:

- Organic milk has higher levels of vitamin E than non-organic

- Organic cheese can have up to twice as many nutrients as non-organic

- Organic wheat, tomatoes, potatoes, cabbage, onions and lettuce have between 20 and 40% more nutrients.

Why does organic food cost more?

Organic foods are more expensive on the whole because they are not mass-produced, and traditional organic farming methods tend to produce lower yields than modern intensive farming. It's worth noting, however, that choosing loose fruit and vegetables over bagged ones (organic or not) is generally better value.

But what about the added cost of organic food? The good news is that, while not competitive with non-organic produce at the moment, prices are definitely getting lower. The growing concern about the quality of the food we feed our children means that more organic food for babies is being sold than ever before, pushing prices down. Sales of organic produce now account for half of the entire baby food market.

Buying fruit and vegetables

When buying fresh fruit and vegetables for your baby or toddler, it may be worth knowing which ones contain more pesticides, on average, than others. A recent study by the Environmental Working Group examined the levels of pesticides in 43 different kinds of fruit and vegetables, based on 43,000 tests.

Mum's top tip

First foods don't have to be complicated or even involve cooking. My son used to love avocado, a very good source of healthy fat, mashed with cottage cheese, a good source of protein. He ate it with a spoon when young and spread it on toast or crackers as he got older. Add mashed banana for a sweeter taste. Simple but highly nutritious!

Those with the highest levels of pesticides included:

- Peaches
- Nectarines
- Cherries
- Grapes
- Sweet peppers
- Apples
- Strawberries
- Lettuce
- Pears

Those with the lowest levels of pesticides included:

- Broccoli
- Asparagus
- Sweetcorn
- Avocados
- Kiwi fruit
- Cabbages
- Peas
- Onions
- Bananas
- Pineapples

Of course, it's not always practical, let alone cost effective, to buy organic. But you can eliminate a lot of the pesticides from non-organic produce simply by washing fresh fruit and vegetables to get rid of any residue left on the skin. Peeling non-organice produce, where feasible, will mean you won't be eating any pesticide left in the skin. It's important to wash organic produce, too, of course, to remove any earth and insects it may have on it.

Growing your own

If you are lucky enough to have a garden in which to grow your own vegetables, or even if you just have a window box, gardening is a great activity for your toddler to get involved in. He will grow up learning about healthy eating and where food comes from. Even if it's just cress grown in a saucer with some cotton wool and water, your child will be fascinated to see what he has planted develop.

First foods for your baby

Mashed avocados or bananas are great first foods for your baby. Let her also try sweet potatoes, carrots and sweet apples or pears. Just cook until soft and then purée in a blender. Baby rice mixed with expressed breast milk or formula can also be a good starter food.

With the best intentions in the world, it will not always be possible to whip up incredible, well-prepared, organic food for your precious infant at the drop of a hat. There will be occasions when you are short of time and need to use pre-prepared food. This is not the end of the world, however, especially during those stressed early months when it may be more practical to feed your baby from a packet or jar from time to time.

However, the more you can manage to make at home yourself, the better. Using fresh ingredients will have a higher nutritional value than food from a packet and is probably going to taste better too.

If you're considering which first foods to try your baby on, you may find the guidelines on pages 106–7 helpful, as they show which foods are appropriate for your baby at each stage of her development. See the guidelines overleaf if you are keen for your baby to be brought up as a vegetarian. Foods to avoid before the age of six months because they are among the most likely to cause an allergic reaction in young children include:

- Eggs
- Nuts and seeds
- Wheat, barley, rye and oats (which contain a protein called gluten)
- Soya
- Dairy products
- Fish and shellfish

The vegetarian baby

It is possible to bring up your baby as a vegetarian so long as you're careful to select a balance of foods that provide sufficient nutrition overall. Too much high-fibre food should be avoided, however, as this will fill her up without supplying all the nutrients she needs.

Iron deficiency is sometimes an issue for vegetarian children, so it's important to give plenty of foods containing iron, such as leafy green vegetables, cereals and eggs. As vitamin C helps to absorb iron, it can be a good idea to give your baby some diluted orange or other fruit juice with meals. (For more on the importance of iron in your child's diet, see pages 116–19.)

Other important food groups are calcium, in cow's milk and other dairy products such as cheese and yoghurt, and vitamins, present in a wide range of fruit and vegetables. It is always best to set up a diet plan for your baby with your health visitor or GP. Likewise, if you want to give your child a vegan diet, in which no dairy produce is present, it is essential you take medical advice in order to ensure she is receiving the best diet for her nutritional needs.

There is quite a wide range of food that your baby can eat if she is vegetarian. However, it's important to remember that some food can cause an allergic reaction and should therefore not be given before the age of six months, at which point your baby's immune system will be more fully developed. (See the list given on page 112.)

AFTER SIX MONTHS
After six months, try your baby on food such as baby rice, millet and maize (all gluten-free), and puréed fruit and vegetables. You could offer her sweet potato, avocado, carrot, swede, butternut squash, apple, pear or banana.

BETWEEN SEVEN AND NINE MONTHS

Between seven and nine months, your baby can eat cereals such as the gluten-free ones listed above. You can also slowly introduce wheat-based products such as cooked pasta shapes, bread and rusks, as well as porridge. And you can try your baby on leafy green vegetables as well as other fruit and vegetables, puréed lentils and mashed potato.

BETWEEN NINE AND 12 MONTHS

Between nine and 12 months, your baby will be getting more and more interested in solid food. Try her on some new things, such as yoghurt, fromage frais and well-cooked eggs. You can also introduce citrus fruit, such such as grapefruit and oranges, kiwi fruit and strawberries (although monitor these carefully as some babies may be allergic to them). Rice cakes, pitta bread and breadsticks all make excellent finger food.

Mum's top tip

We are very happy with our decision to bring up our daughter as a veggie, and hope to raise a strong-minded individual who makes her own choices just like I did – deciding to become vegetarian at the age of seven. Starting on solids is very messy but great fun: our daughter is beautiful, healthy and the cheekiest monkey ever and I believe that is because she eats good, home-cooked veggie meals. I'm sure your little one will be the same.

The importance of iron for babies and toddlers

Iron is extremely important for growing babies and toddlers. It enables blood to store oxygen so that it can be delivered to every part of the body. In a young child, it is essential for the proper development and function of the nerves, muscles and brain.

It is recommended that babies under 12 months have 11mg of iron a day; while children aged one to three years need 7mg. Before birth your baby will have built up supplies of iron while in the womb. This means that your diet during pregnancy is very important. Pregnant women are advised to eat an iron-rich diet. Red meat is the best source, while vegetarians can get iron from bread, pulses and green vegetables such as watercress, broccoli and spring greens. (See the list overleaf for more iron-rich sources of food.)

Premature or low-birthweight babies are at increased risk of iron deficiency and may need iron supplements (given under medical supervision only).

When your baby is born, he will have enough iron stored in his body to last the first 4–6 months of his life. After this time, he'll need to get iron from the food he eats. Breast milk contains iron that babies can easily absorb, but there's not enough to meet a child's increasing demands. When your baby is weaning, be sure to choose iron-rich baby foods by checking the ingredients carefully, or make your own baby food to ensure he gets enough iron.

The Department of Health recommends not giving cow's milk (which is low in iron) as the main drink before 12 months of age; bottlefed babies should be given fortified formula milk.

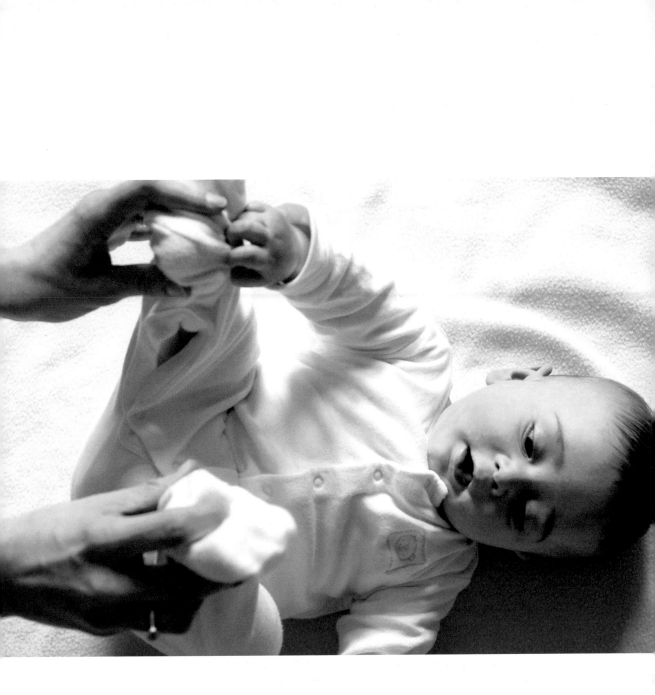

Iron-rich foods

- Liver (or liver pâté), but only serve once a week
- Lean beef, chicken and pork
- Seafood, especially canned tuna and salmon
- Leafy greens, including spinach and kale
- Other vegetables, including broccoli, parsley, watercress, Brussels sprouts and Swiss chard
- Tofu, soya beans and cooked dried beans
- Nuts
- Eggs
- Dried fruit, such as raisins, prunes, dates and apricots

Vitamin C and iron absorption

Vitamin C enhances iron absorption, so serve your baby vitamin C-rich foods alongside iron-rich ones. These include:

- Strawberries
- Blackcurrants
- Tomatoes
- Sweet potatoes
- Kiwi fruit
- Sweet peppers
- Cabbage and broccoli
- Citrus fruit, such as oranges and grapefruit
- Melons

Bear in mind, however, that some foods may cause an allergic reaction (see the list on page 112) and that it's best to proceed carefully when introducing new foods to your baby.

Avoiding anaemia

If your baby is eating a balanced diet consisting of a variety of foods from the first list opposite, supplemented by foods from the second list, he is probably getting enough iron. Too much iron (for example, if your baby is given iron supplements when already eating a balanced diet) can be dangerous.

If your baby's store of iron is low and there is too little in the diet to form new red blood cells, symptoms of anaemia will start to develop. If your child is lacking in iron, he may display some or all of the following symptoms:

- Weakness
- Paleness
- Rapid heartbeat or a new heart murmur (detected in an examination by your child's doctor)
- Irritability
- Decreased appetite
- Dizziness

If you have any concerns that your child isn't getting enough iron, consult your GP.

cook's tip

Creamy Spinach Pasta is delicious, easy to make and provides my little one with lots of fabulous iron and healthy fats. Shred a few handfuls of washed spinach and wilt in a saucepan with a little boiled water. Drain and stir through cream (double cream works best) until the spinach is sauce-like in consistency. Heat through and pour over cooked pasta. For babies, you can blitz the spinach in a blender.

Baby-feeding dos and don'ts

When you're thinking of introducing solid food into your baby's diet, the first thing to consider is what foods to try.

It can be very tempting to rush into the kitchen and start conjuring up exotic combinations of fruit and vegetables as an introduction to the exciting world of food, but in reality you should probably limit the purées you make to a single ingredient, which will mean you can establish how popular each new food is with your baby. There will be time for more lavish dishes later.

Use organic fruit and vegetables where possible as they will be additive-free and tasty to boot. Making food for your baby is also much cheaper than buying it in a shop, so it's worth spending a bit of time every week making up some purées. You can always freeze them (health visitors often recommend using an ice-cube tray for freezing separate portions) and use them during the course of the week.

In the beginning, it might be an idea to give your baby half of her usual milk feed before you try her on something new. That way, she won't be over-hungry, nor will she be too full. Try not to pick a time when she is fractious (perhaps due to fatigue) and try to establish a routine by feeding her at the same time each day. Lunchtime may be good for this.

The best place for this feeding ritual is probably in your kitchen (close to a good supply of kitchen towels and wet cloths!) and in a highchair. To begin with, you may want to have her on your lap, but you can only do that for so long before she gets too big and you get too messy.

At first she will probably only eat a teaspoonful or so. You can offer her more, but if she loses interest, it is probably best to carry on with the rest of her milk feed.

Babies have to learn how to swallow (hence the dribbling and regurgitation that turns you, her and the surrounding area into a Jackson Pollock painting), so be patient. For the first couple of months, at least, you need to become accustomed to your lovingly blended vegetable concoctions being unceremoniously spat out as your baby learns her craft.

If your baby truly shows no interest in food, then it is prudent to leave weaning for a bit longer before trying again. Keep up the usual milk feeds and perhaps try something a bit blander: breast milk and baby rice or puréed potato. It could be the strong taste of the new food that your baby is rejecting. Whatever the reason, your baby will eventually show interest in eating. Some babies just take longer over the weaning process than others.

Mum's top tip

When I introduced new foods into my baby's diet, I did it gradually – a new food every three days or so – and kept a food diary to track what my baby ate and when. If a particular food didn't meet with her approval, I'd note it down, avoid it for a few months, then try it again when my baby was a little older.

Top tips for weaning your baby

- **Do** try single ingredients at first. This will help you to find out which flavours your baby enjoys and which ones she doesn't like. You'll also be able to identify more easily any foods to which she may be intolerant or allergic. (For a list of likely candidates, see page 112.)

- **Do** try and buy organic food if you can, or if that isn't feasible, then make sure the skin of non-organic fruit and vegetables is removed first wherever possible to get rid of any harmful residues. (For more on the benefits of buying organic, see pages 108–11.)

- **Do** invest in a good highchair if you can; this will make feeding time a lot easier.

- **Don't** use unsterilized bowls and spoons when you first start feeding your baby.

- **Don't** use shop-bought jars if you can avoid it: homemade food will be more nutritious and much tastier for your baby.

- **Do** stock up with plenty of washable bibs, kitchen towels and cloths. This will help decrease the likelihood of your kitchen looking like a war zone!

- **Don't** panic, if at first your baby doesn't seem interested in food: she will show you when she is ready and until that point she will be receiving all the nutrition that she needs from her usual milk feeds.

top
tips

Watch out for salt in your baby's diet

Babies require far less salt in their diet than adults do. This is because their developing organs cannot cope with the same levels of salt as adults. This applies particularly to the kidneys, which regulate the salt and water content in the body.

WHY IS IT SO IMPORTANT TO AVOID ADDING SALT TO BABY FOOD?

The NHS states that while your baby's organs and digestive system are still developing, it is important not to add any extra salt to her food. You should also be careful not to feed her ordinary processed foods, instead sticking to specially-formulated baby foods. This is because many processed foods already have a high salt content. Salt can be 'hidden' in many ready-made foods, such as bread, baked beans and even biscuits, and so it can be easy to ingest too much. Babies who are breastfed get just the right amount of salt through breast milk. Infant formula milk contains a similar amount of salt to breast milk, so until your baby moves on to solids you can't go far wrong.

WHAT ARE THE SYMPTOMS OF SALT OVERDOSE?

When there is too much salt in the body, fluid is drawn from the cells, making them shrivel up. This can be dangerous for a baby and could, potentially, lead to brain damage. If your baby is pale and has sunken eyes, it could be a sign that she is dehydrated (see pages 80–84). You may also notice that she is urinating less than usual. A good check is to see if the soft spot, or fontanelle, on your baby's head is sunken. More serious symptoms include fits or seizures and even coma.

All about baby-led weaning

Baby-led weaning (also known as BLW) is a gradual method of weaning that helps babies move from milk to a solid diet. Here are the basic principles.

Once your baby has reached the right stage developmentally to start on solids (aged six months), you can offer him a range of different finger foods (from various food groups), rather than the puréed first foods which are recommended by most postnatal healthcare providers.

Your child is therefore encouraged to self-feed rather than you feeding him. At first he may just lick the food, but the important thing is that he is in control: he decides when to try what you have presented to him. The idea is that this will help him to be independent about the feeding process. As long as he has developed the pincer grasp (picking things up with his thumb and forefinger), he should be able to hold onto finger foods.

Your baby is allowed to decide how much food he eats or does not eat. If he rejects food, it can be offered again later on. Water is also offered with the meal and pieces of food should not be bite-sized but baton-sized, thus allowing your baby to grab on properly and get a good hold.

Obviously, you shouldn't offer food that has added sugar or salt or is potentially a choking hazard, such as peanuts.

As this is still a relatively new method of weaning, you should inform your health visitor if you'd like to try it so that she can give you more information.

Weaning off the breast

If you're interested in baby-led weaning, you may find the following information on weaning off the breast helpful:

1 Pick your moment

It's best not to start weaning your baby from your breast if something is happening that might be upsetting his usual routine. This might be as traumatic as a move to a new house or, on a lesser scale, cutting a new tooth. Either way, such events can be stressful for a little person and getting rid of a good comforter such as breastfeeding is only going to make your job harder.

2 Take one step at a time

Unless you have been instructed by your GP to stop breastfeeding quickly (perhaps prior to being admitted to hospital), then you should finish gradually rather than coming to a sudden, screeching halt. Your baby will be able to cope with the change if it is approached in the right way. Cut down on the breastfeeding little by little: pick one feed to cut out (preferably one that doesn't seem very important in an emotional sense to your child) and do without this one for a good few days, preferably a week, before cutting out another.

3 Express a little milk

In order to minimize any physical discomfort, you should express a little milk. However, don't express more than you need to feel comfortable, as your breasts will keep making the same amount of milk. You should express some, though, as otherwise your breasts could become engorged and possibly develop mastitis (see page 47).

g For the **gurgle** video on **Pumping and expressing**, go to **gurgle.com** and click on **Videos**

4 Offer substitutes

If your baby is under 12 months, don't forget he needs either breast or formula milk to satisfy his nutritional needs, so do encourage him to take a bottle. (For information on making up a bottle, see page 59.)

5 Ask for help

You may need support at this time, from your partner or a relative or friend. If your partner has been giving your baby bottles (either of your expressed milk or of formula), then the chances are that weaning will be less of an ordeal for everyone involved. He will already have helped to make clear to your baby that it is not only you who is able to provide feeds. To stop giving a bedtime feed, it can be necessary to ask your partner or relative to take over bedtimes for a while, in order to introduce a 'new' breastless routine.

6 The art of distraction

You will already be a veteran of baby-focused distraction techniques and this will be the ultimate test of your skills. Get out, get walking, go to the park, go swimming – in short, do whatever it takes to occupy your baby. No time to think about breastfeeding can only be a good thing. Sitting down with him is an open invitation for a quick snack.

Above all, make sure that your baby receives lots of hugs and kisses and is made to feel very loved. This is a big change for him and he may feel slightly insecure or vulnerable. If you are finding this process of weaning your baby from the breast difficult, don't hesitate to seek support. Organizations such as the National Childbirth Trust (see 'Resources', pages 216–17, for contact details), will be able to give you lots of help and advice on a wide range of breastfeeding-related questions.

top tips

Mum's top tip

My advice is to tune in to your baby to see if he's ready for solids. If he starts watching you with interest when you eat – or even reaching out for your food – that's usually a sign that he's ready. My son started to wake in the night at about five and a half months, so I started weaning him slowly and he soon settled again and started sleeping through, so he was obviously hungry!

Your baby's feeding routine: six to nine months

By the time your baby reaches six months, she may well have doubled her birth weight and be having four milk feeds and two to three meals plus snacks a day. At around this age, most babies start becoming used to a variety of solid foods, particularly infant cereal, fruit and vegetables.

You may find your baby isn't quite so keen on meat at first, but fortunately she doesn't need a lot – around 25g (1oz) a day is enough. Tofu or pulses such as lentils, beans or chickpeas are also packed with protein and your baby might prefer the taste and texture of them.

You should still be breastfeeding your baby, or bottlefeeding her with iron-fortified infant formula, continuing to do so until she's 12 months of age. A typical feeding routine for a baby of 6–9 months is suggested opposite.

If your baby is gnawing anything she can get her sticky little mitts on, it's more than likely a sign that she's getting ready to teethe. Your baby needs to develop her chewing skills, so you shouldn't be puréeing food by this stage but mashing it instead with a fork or dicing it finely so it has a coarser texture.

Always give your baby full-fat as opposed to low-fat dairy products (cheese, yoghurt, etc). She needs the fat to enable her brain to develop. It's fine to give your baby small tastes of dairy products such as cheese after six months, provided there is no family history of eczema or dairy allergy. (For more on allergies, see pages 162–9.)

Typical feeding routine

6.30am Breast- or bottlefeed (200–225ml/7–8oz).

8am Breakfast: stewed or soft fruit and yoghurt, toast fingers, breakfast cereal. (Only give your baby breakfast cereal that is labelled as being suitable for babies. Many adult breakfast cereals have a high salt content which could be dangerous for infants.)

8.30am Breast- or bottlefeed.

12pm Lunch: finely chopped vegetables, beans, lentils or tofu; minced pasta/rice with fresh tomato sauce; scrambled egg yolks. (Only serve your baby eggs yolks – egg whites contain potential allergens. If there is a history of allergy in the family, delay the introduction of eggs until after 12 months of age.)

12.30pm Breast- or bottlefeed.

5pm Dinner: finely chopped moist chicken or fish (with all bones removed) served with mashed vegetables; custard and stewed/soft fruit.

7pm Breast- or bottlefeed.

Recipes from six months

Butternut squash purée

Butternut squash and pumpkins can be made into a wonderfully smooth purée, making them ideal first foods. Their vibrant orange colour also makes them eye-catching and appealing to a baby. If freezing the purée, serve just 1–2 defrosted ice cube sized portions as an introduction to weaning.

Preparation time 10 minutes
Cooking time 15 minutes
Freezing suitable
Makes 225ml (8fl oz) or 12 frozen cubes

225g (8oz) butternut squash
4 tablespoons formula or breast milk or cooled, boiled water

1 Peel the squash, cut in half and and remove the seeds. Put the flesh into a sieve and rinse with cooled, boiled water, drain and dice then add to the top of a steamer. Cover and put over a saucepan of boiling water. Steam for 15 minutes until tender.

2 Transfer to a liquidizer then purée, gradually adding the milk or water, until smooth and soup-like in consistency. Press through a sieve to make sure it is completely lump free. Serve a portion now (checking the temperature before serving) and spoon the rest into sections of an ice-cube tray. Cover the tray and chill, then freeze until required.

cook's tip If you don't have a liquidizer, then simply mash the cooked squash with a fork before pressing it through a sieve to get rid of any lumps.

Winter harvest

Once your baby has tried a few single-ingredient meals, you may feel he is now ready to move on to a simple vegetable blend. As long as you keep to the same total vegetable weight, the actual amounts can be varied to suit whatever you have to hand, adding perhaps some sweet potato or butternut squash in place of the parsnip or carrot. Due to their starchy nature and the fact that they don't have many nutrients, some nutritionists suggest not introducing standard white potatoes into your baby's diet until he is 8–10 months old. But as sweet potato is high in vitamin C, it's fine to introduce this earlier.

Preparation time 10 minutes
Cooking time 20 minutes
Freezing suitable
Makes 400ml (14fl oz) or 20 frozen cubes

100g (4oz) parsnips
100g (4oz) carrots
100g (4oz) potatoes (or butternut squash or swede)
150ml (¹/₄ pint) formula or breast milk or cooled, boiled water

1 Peel the vegetables, place in a sieve and then rinse away any traces of soil with cooled, boiled water. Drain and dice. Add to the top of a steamer, cover and put over a saucepan of boiling water. Steam for about 20 minutes until tender.

2 Transfer to a liquidizer, then purée, gradually adding the milk or water, until smooth and soup-like in consistency. Press through a sieve to make sure it is lump free. Serve a portion now (checking the temperature just before serving), spooning the rest into sections of an ice-cube tray. Cover the tray and chill, then freeze until required.

cook's tip

Instead of a steamer, you can use a sieve set over a pan of boiling water with a piece of foil as a lid. The vegetables can also be boiled, although this will lower the vitamin and mineral content.

Pear purée

Cook fruit in the first stages of weaning and make sure to sieve out any lumps so that it is easier for your baby to digest. Resist the temptation to add sugar or honey, opting for just-ripe pears for maximum natural sweetness. For an apple purée, simply substitute the same weight of pears for a naturally sweet apple such as Gala rather than the more tangy Braeburn or Granny Smith.

Preparation time 10 minutes
Cooking time 10 minutes
Freezing suitable
Makes 225ml (8fl oz) or 12 frozen cubes

300g (11oz) or 2 just-ripe pears
3 tablespoons boiled water

1 Wash the pears with cooled, boiled water from the kettle, then peel, core and dice. Add to a saucepan with the 3 tablespoons of boiled water, cover and cook gently for 10 minutes until soft.

2 Transfer to a liquidizer and purée until smooth, then press through a sieve to make sure it is lump free. Adjust the consistency if needed with a little extra cooled, boiled water. Spoon a portion into a bowl to serve now (checking the temperature before serving) and the rest into sections of an ice-cube tray. Cover and then freeze until required.

cook's tip Once weaning has been in progress for 3–4 weeks your baby's tummy will have adjusted to the move from milk to a more varied diet and will be able to digest a purée made with uncooked ripe pears.

Apple rice pudding

This can be a great stepping stone from the milky taste that your baby has been used to over the previous 6 months. Here baby rice is mixed with ultra-smooth apple purée for a delicately fruity flavour.

Preparation time 10 minutes
Cooking time 8–10 minutes
Freezing not suitable
Makes 150ml ($1/4$ pint) or 2–3 portions

1 Gala dessert apple
1 tablespoon pure baby rice
3 tablespoons formula or breast milk or cooled, boiled water

1 Wash the apple with cooled, boiled water from the kettle, then peel, core and dice. Put into the top of a steamer, cover and cook over a saucepan of boiling water for 8–10 minutes until tender. Or put into a microwave-proof bowl with 1 tablespoon of cooled boiled water. Cover with a plate and microwave on full power for $1^{1}/_{2}$–2 minutes.

2 Press the cooked apple through a sieve to make a smooth purée.

3 Put the baby rice into a bowl and mix in milk or water until smooth (or follow pack instructions). Stir in the puréed apple. Adjust the consistency to suit your baby with a little extra milk or cooled boiled water, if needed. Spoon a portion into a bowl to serve now (checking the temperature before serving) and the rest into a second bowl. Cover and chill until required.

cook's tip

To make your own baby rice, put 1 tablespoon of organic risotto, basmati or long-grain white rice into a sieve, rinse with boiled water and drain. Bring 150ml ($1/4$ pint) water to the boil, add the rice, then simmer for 12–15 minutes until very soft. Purée in a liquidizer then press through a sieve until smooth. Adjust the thickness if needed with a little cooled formula or breast milk. This will make two portions. Cover and chill the remaining portion in the fridge overnight.

Recipes from seven to nine months

Banana and apple porridge

Although we traditionally think of porridge as being made with oats, millet flakes, available from health-food shops, make not only a speedier breakfast but one that is also gluten-free and contains silicon, needed for healthy bones, teeth, nails and hair. The second portion of porridge could be served to a toddler.

Preparation time 5 minutes
Cooking time 3–4 minutes
Freezing not suitable
Makes 200ml (7floz) or 2 servings

1 Gala dessert apple
1 small ripe banana
150ml (¼ pint) formula or breast milk
2 tablespoons millet flakes

1 Wash the apple with cooled, boiled water, then peel, core and coarsely grate. Peel and dice the banana. Pour the milk into a small saucepan, bring to the boil, then add the millet flakes, apple and banana. Simmer for 4–5 minutes, stirring from time to time, until the millet flakes and fruit are very soft.

2 Mash the porridge into a coarse purée or a finer one, to suit your baby. Spoon a portion into a bowl to serve now (checking the temperature before serving) and the remainder into a second bowl. Cover and chill until required.

cook's
tip

The longer the porridge stands, the thicker it will become, so adjust the consistency as needed with a little extra cooled, boiled water or formula milk.

Courgette and sweet potato purée

Just like adults, many babies prefer sweet flavours to savoury ones. To encourage your baby not to acquire a sweet tooth, dilute the flavour of sweet potato with the delicate taste of courgette.

Preparation time 10 minutes
Cooking time 25 minutes
Freezing suitable
Makes 600ml (1 pint) or 6 servings

300g (11oz) or 1 medium sweet potato
225g (8oz) or 2 courgettes
150ml (¼ pint) formula or breast milk or cooled, boiled water

1 Peel the sweet potato, then rinse this and the courgettes with cooled, boiled water. Drain and then dice each separately. Put the sweet potato into the top of a steamer, cover and place over a saucepan of boiling water. Steam for 15 minutes. Add the courgettes and steam for 8–10 minutes more until tender.

2 Transfer to a liquidizer, then purée, gradually adding the milk or water, until very smooth. Serve a portion now (checking the temperature before serving), leaving the rest to cool. Spoon into sections of an ice-cube tray or small freezer containers. Cover and freeze until required.

cook's tip

Once weaning is fully established, reduce the amount of liquid slightly or swap a little of the liquid for a spoonful of mascarpone or full-fat cream cheese – providing that there is no family history of asthma, eczema or other dairy allergies – and mash the vegetables for a coarser texture.

Baby carrot and sweet potato dhal

Don't be put off if your child refuses something new. Offer a food he will eat and then try the new food again a few days or weeks later.

Preparation time 10 minutes
Cooking time 25 minutes
Freezing suitable
Makes 450ml (³/₄ pint) or 4–5 servings

150g (5oz) or 1 carrot
225g (8oz) or 1 medium sweet potato
40g (1¹/₂oz) red lentils
Large pinch ground turmeric
Large pinch ground cumin
300ml (¹/₂ pint) homemade vegetable or chicken stock or water
1 tomato

1 Peel the carrot and sweet potato, rinse off any traces of soil with cooled, boiled water from the kettle and then dice.

2 Put the vegetables into a saucepan with the lentils, spices and stock. Bring to the boil, then cover and simmer for 25 minutes until the lentils and vegetables are very soft.

3 Meanwhile, make a cross cut in the tomato and put into a bowl of boiling water. Wait 1 minute, then lift out, peel off the skin, scoop out the seeds and finely dice the flesh.

4 Transfer the lentil mixture to a liquidizer, add the tomato and mix to a coarse purée, or roughly mash to a texture to suit your baby. Adjust the consistency with a little extra boiled water, if needed. Spoon a portion into a bowl to serve now (checking the temperature before serving), leaving the rest to cool. Spoon into sections of an ice-cube tray or small freezer containers. Cover and freeze until required.

cook's tip It's important not to use stock made with bought stock cubes. Even those with a reduced salt content are still too strong for your baby's kidneys to cope with.

Chicken hotpot

Now that your baby's natural iron stores have been used up, boost vital supplies by putting a little meat on the menu.

Preparation time 15 minutes
Cooking time 45 minutes
Freezing suitable
Makes 600ml (1 pint) or 6 servings

150g (5oz) or 1 boneless, skinless chicken breast
100g (4oz) parsnip or swede
150g (5oz) or 1 carrot
200g (7oz) or 2 small potatoes
1 spring onion, trimmed
1 sprig fresh rosemary
300ml ($^1/_2$ pint) homemade chicken or vegetable stock or water

1 Rinse the chicken breast with cooled, boiled water from the kettle, then dice. Peel the root vegetables, then rinse off any soil residue from these, the spring onion and rosemary with boiled water. Thinly slice the spring onion and dice the root vegetables.

2 Heat a little olive oil in a small, flameproof casserole dish, add the chicken and spring onion and stir fry for 4-5 minutes until just beginning to brown. Add the remaining vegetables, rosemary sprig and stock or water. Bring to the boil, then cover and simmer for 40 minutes until the vegetables are tender and the chicken thoroughly cooked.

3 Mash, finely chop or liquidize the hotpot until a coarse purée to suit your baby. Spoon a portion into a bowl to serve now (checking the temperature before serving), leaving the rest to cool. Spoon into an ice cube tray or small freezer containers. Cover and freeze until required.

cook's tip

If it suits you better, then make up this dish in a flameproof casserole dish, cover and transfer to an oven preheated to 180°C (350°F), Gas 4 for 1 hour.

Broccoli and butternut squash risotto

Giving softly cooked rice in a risotto is a good way of encouraging your baby to try food that has a little texture. Even without teeth, he may be able to manage to chew soft lumps, which in turn will help develop the muscles involved with speech.

Preparation time 10 minutes
Cooking time 19–20 minutes
Freezing suitable
Makes 400ml (14fl oz) or 4 servings

150g (5oz) butternut squash
1 spring onion, trimmed
50g (2oz) broccoli
75g (3oz) Arborio rice
200ml (7fl oz) formula or breast milk
200–225ml (7–8fl oz) homemade vegetable stock
or boiled water

1 Peel the squash, cut it in half and remove the seeds, then rinse this, the spring onion and broccoli with cooled, boiled water from the kettle. Dice the squash, slice the onion and chop the broccoli.

2 Add the squash and onion to a small saucepan, add the rice, milk and 200ml (7fl oz) of the stock or boiled water. Bring to the boil, then simmer for 15 minutes, stirring from time to time, until the rice is almost tender.

3 Add the broccoli and a little extra stock or water, if needed. Cook for 4–5 minutes, stirring more frequently as the mixture thickens, until the vegetables and rice are soft.

4 Mash, chop or liquidize the risotto to suit your baby. Serve a portion now (checking the temperature before serving), leaving the rest to cool. Spoon into an ice-cube tray or small freezer containers, Cover and freeze until required.

Tropical fruit crush

Packed with taste, not to mention vitamin C, this healthy and speedy pud is a great way to broaden your baby's tastes. Try with mashed papaya and melon or mashed banana and blueberries.

Preparation time 10 minutes
Cooking time none
Freezing not suitable
Makes 225ml (8fl oz) or 3 servings

1 small ripe mango
1 Charentais or Galia melon

Remove the stone and peel from the mango and the peel and seeds from the melon. Crush the fruit with a fork on a large plate or liquidize to a coarse purée.

Snacks and drinks

At around seven to eight months your baby will start to pick things up with her thumb and finger and transfer them from one hand to another. Once she has reached this stage, it's a good idea to encourage her to start feeding herself by offering finger foods as snacks.

These can include: toasted bread, roti, naan or bagels, bite-sized pieces of cheese or fruit, tiny sandwiches filled with soft cheese or mashed banana, cubes of tofu.

What to avoid

Avoid, as far as possible, giving sugary foods such as cake or biscuits. And if you give jars of baby food to your child, whether as a meal or a snack, always read the labels to avoid unnecessary ingredients such as starch and sugar, bearing in mind that the first ingredient on any food label is the one it contains in the largest amount.

Water is best

Water is by far the healthiest and purest drink (not including milk) you can offer your baby. Now that she is weaned, offer water whenever she is thirsty but not due a feed. Try to stick to water as your baby's main drink for as long as you can. Although rich in vitamin C, fruit juice can reduce your baby's appetite for milk. It also contains natural sugars and acids which can cause tooth decay.

If you do want to give juice, always dilute one part juice with five parts cooled, boiled water, and serve in a cup, never a bottle, to minimize the risk of tooth decay. Finally, never give your baby any of the following: juice drinks that are not pure fruit juice; sugary or fizzy drinks; drinks described as 'low-calorie' or 'with no added sugar'; flavoured milk or water; tea, coffee or herbal drinks.

Preparing baby food safely

When preparing food for your baby, common sense prevails, as ever. Make sure you wash your hands properly and wash her hands too, as she will be putting her hands near and in her mouth.

You can buy weaning spoons and bowls made of soft plastic, which will be suitable for feeding your baby with at first. These spoons are shallow with long handles and the bowl may a have suction grip on the bottom, thus reducing the possibility of your lovingly prepared food being hurled across the kitchen.

All this feeding equipment should be washed in water at a temperature above 80°C (176°F) to ensure that it is sterile. If you are using baby food from a jar, it is best to put a portion of it into a bowl rather than the whole lot. If your baby hasn't eaten all of the food in her bowl, throw the leftovers away as saliva can mix with it, potentially breeding germs and making it unsuitable for eating later.

Here are some simple hygiene rules for you to follow when preparing baby foods and feeds:

- Once opened, store any jars of baby food in the fridge and use within 48 hours

- Regularly wipe kitchen equipment, highchairs and work surfaces

- Always check use-by dates and stick to them rigorously when preparing food for young children

- Check that the seals on food and jars haven't been broken before using the food

- Don't leave food in opened cans – always throw leftovers away

- Defrost frozen foods thoroughly and read the defrosting guides on food labels

- Always cook eggs so that they are well done

- Heat food so that it is piping hot, then let it cool down

- Always taste food first to check it is at the right temperature for your baby. Remember that food heated in a microwave can have hot spots that could burn your baby's mouth, so make sure it has sufficiently cooled all the way through

- Keep bottles of breast milk in the fridge before feeding (and then warm to the desired temperature)

- Never microwave your baby's milk bottles as 'hot spots' can occur and cause her to burn her mouth. Place bottles in cooling boiled water to warm them up

- Store puréed fruits or vegetables for 2–3 days in the fridge or for 6–8 months in the freezer

- Store prepared dishes containing meat or eggs for one day in the fridge and 1–2 months in the freezer.

Is it safe to give my baby food from a jar?

The European Food Safety Authority (EFSA) recently raised the alarm after finding a carcinogenic toxin called semicarbazide (SEM) in a range of products, including baby food. The toxin, which has been linked to cancer in animals, appeared to be getting into the baby food through the plastic gaskets used to seal glass jars with metal twist-off lids. The EFSA has made it clear that the health risks are low. 'The risk to consumers resulting from the possible presence of semicarbazide in foods, if any, is judged to be very small, not only for adults but also for infants,' says EFSA scientist Dr Sue Barlow.

Martin Paterson, deputy director-general of the UK's Food and Drink Federation, has said that a joint food and packaging industry taskforce is working with the authorities to eliminate SEM from the metal twist caps used with glass jars. It is unclear whether this has been implemented across the board, but current advice is that it is safe to feed babies from jars. If you are concerned about this issue, then you may want to use baby food from packets instead.

top
tips

Reducing night feeding

It's a question that many a sleep-deprived first-time mum asks: 'When will my baby sleep through the night?' Of course, we've all heard stories of those marvellously considerate babies who sleep through from ten until six from the word go, but the reality is that most small babies simply aren't able to go for long stretches at night without a feed.

However, by the age of six months your baby should have a more established sleeping pattern and should be able to sleep through from 11 or 12 at night until five or six in the morning. Many parents see a big improvement in their babies' sleeping paterns once they are on solid food. Feeling fuller, they don't wake so often during the night to feed. So why is your baby still waking in the night? The chances are he isn't really hungry but there is some other factor which is disrupting his sleep.

Why does my baby wake in the night?

1 He can't settle himself back to sleep
Many babies find it hard to settle themselves back to sleep and get into the habit of nodding off while having that last breastfeed at night. You can help to wean him off this habit by not letting him fall asleep on the breast when you put him down, maybe playing some music instead or reading a story after his last feed. The more he gets used to going off to sleep without Mummy, the easier it will be for him to do so when he wakes in the night.

2 He's got into the habit of waking at that time
Even grown-ups find that sometimes they go through a phase of waking at the same time every night. If your baby has been

waking routinely for feeds in the night, it may well have become a habit which you need to try and gently break. If you are sure that he isn't really hungry, try and get your baby used to settling himself back to sleep instead of having a breastfeed.

3 He's teething
Teething babies tend to wake more frequently in the night simply due to the discomfort they are experiencing. A little infant ibuprofen or paracetamol should help to take the edge off the pain and make it easier for your baby to sleep. Always remember to read the label and administer the right dose for your baby's age.

4 He's got a cold or a temperature
Similarly, if your baby has a runny nose or a temperature, he'll be more likely to wake in the night, and there's little you can do except to give medication to try and bring down his temperature if he has one. Check that he's not dedydrated, giving him some water if necessary.

5 He's genuinely hungry
Of course, don't discount the obvious. He may well be genuinely hungry, in which case you might want to try and give a slightly larger feed before he goes to sleep in the hope that this will tide him over. Some babies simply have large appetites and even the onset of solids might not be enough to get them through the night. Formula-fed babies tend to sleep through more readily than breastfed ones, simply because breast milk, being easier to digest, passes through their system more quickly. So if you are feeding your baby a mixture of breast and bottle, you may find that a formula feed last thing at night fills him up enough to enable him to sleep through.

Do babies and toddlers need vitamin supplements?

According to the most recent advice from the Food Standards Agency (FSA), children between the ages of six months and five years who do not eat a varied and healthy diet will benefit from taking drops containing vitamins A, C and D.

This, the FSA says, will help ensure that even if a child doesn't get the nutrients she needs from her diet, she'll still get all the vitamins she requires.

Vitamin drops are free for children under five in families receiving income support or income-based job seeker's allowance. They can also be bought cheaply from child health clinics.

However, if your child has a hearty appetite and eats a wide variety of foods, including plenty of fresh fruit and vegetables, she may not need vitamin supplements.

Good sources of A, C and D

VITAMIN A
- Milk
- Eggs
- Liver
- Fortified cereals
- Orange-coloured fruits and vegetables, such as peaches, apricots, mangoes, sweet potatoes, carrots and pumpkins
- Green vegetables, such as spinach, cabbage and kale

VITAMIN C

- Guava
- Broccoli
- Strawberries
- Cauliflower
- Spinach
- Raspberries
- Red/yellow peppers
- Kiwi fruit
- Papaya
- Oranges
- Grapefruit
- Cabbage
- Tangerines

VITAMIN D

Vitamin D is essential for normal growth and development. It helps the body absorb calcium, which is important for the development of strong bones. A child deficient in vitamin D is at risk of weakened bones and stunted growth. Severe and prolonged vitamin D deficiency can cause rickets, a bone-weakening disease normally associated with developing countries, where poor nutrition is common.

There aren't many food sources of vitamin D, oily fish, liver and egg yolks being the only foods that contain it naturally. However, certain foods are fortified with vitamin D, including milk, soya drinks, margarine and some cereals.

A healthy, balanced diet will provide some vitamin D, but regular exposure to sunlight – around ten minutes a day (although of course you must make sure that your child's skin is protected with a suitable sunscreen) – is necessary to help your child formulate enough of the vitamin.

If your child doesn't spend much time outdoors or wears clothes that cover most of her skin when outside, and if she doesn't get a good supply from her diet, you may want to consider giving her a vitamin D supplement. Young babies are more likely to need a supplement because they have very little exposure to the sunshine. Always speak to your GP or health visitor before giving a vitamin supplement to your child.

Learning to drink from a cup

Getting your baby to drink from a cup when he's accustomed to drinking from a bottle can be a bit of a struggle. If you try once and he's resistant to it, you may need to persist or try again a week or so later.

The earlier you introduce your baby to a cup, the better, as the longer you leave it the more attached he will become to his bottle. In general, babies can try a cup at six months and be weaned off the bottle around 12–18 months. Babies who are ready to be weaned can sit up by themselves; are able to eat from a spoon; have a regular feeding routine; and show more interest in solid foods.

As a rule, it's recommended that babies don't drink from a bottle past the age of one. Not only is drinking from a teat linked to tooth decay, a child who depends on bottle feeds may not consume enough food to meet his nutritional requirements.

Start around six to nine months

It's up to you when you decide to try your baby on a cup for the first time, but it might be worth offering one when he's around six months old to see if he will drink from it. While some babies take to it straight away and find it just as easy to drink from a cup as from a bottle, others might be more resistant because it feels so different to drinking from a bottle.

Experiment with different types of cup

You may have to try a variety of cups before you find one your baby is happy with. There are transitional or 'trainer' cups which still resemble bottles and may therefore seem more familiar to your child. They have a gentle, more flexible spout, similar to the teat of a bottle, and so won't feel so rigid in your baby's mouth.

There are also non-spill or 'sippy' cups, which are very popular with parents for obvious reasons. However, your baby will have to suck harder to get the liquid out and may become frustrated, so this might not necessarily be the best cup on which to start him.

So, if you've been resolutely trying to get your baby to drink from a cup of the non-spill variety and he's struggling, bear in mind that there are other easier types of cup to try. You could, for example, offer your baby his drink in an open cup where the liquid is readily accessible. He may be more receptive to this idea, as it's how Mummy and Daddy drink; he can copy you and feel like a grown-up!

When attempting to get your baby to drink from a cup, try not to worry about the mess. The important thing is for your baby to get the hang of taking liquid out of something other than a bottle, and a few spillages along the way are to be expected as he adjusts.

Remember that there's no set age at which your child should drink from a cup, but obviously you will want to wean him off his bottle at some point. If you can introduce a cup before your child is one – whether it's a trainer, non-spill or open cup – so much the better.

Mum's top tip

When helping my son, aged 11 months, to learn to drink from a cup with a soft spout, I find the best times of day to try are lunchtime and late afternoon, after he's eaten some solid food, is more thirsty and needs more liquid than he would after a milk feed. It's also best to start off with plain water in the cup.

Moving on: 9–12 months

Your baby's feeding routine: 9–12 months

If he hasn't already, your baby is probably ready to leave the smooth purées behind and start tucking into food with much more texture.

He may well have a few teeth by now, and will be able to eat larger pieces of a greater variety of foods. He will probably be much more proficient at chewing. He may want to eat with his fingers (and will try to grab whatever you're eating from your hand!) or a spoon, and he can drink from a cup, possibly even holding it himself.

Typical feeding routine

Stick to three main meals a day with healthy snacks in between.

Breakfast 3-5 tablespoons of iron-fortified baby cereal with 175-225ml (6-8fl oz) of breast milk or formula.

Lunch 3-4 tablespoons cooked vegetables.

Dinner 3-4 tablespoons of cooked vegetables; 3-4 tablespoons of minced or diced cooked meat, tofu, beans or eggs; 3-4 tablespoons fruit; 175-225ml (6-8fl oz) of breast milk or formula.

Recipes for 9–12 months

Mini oven-baked frittata

Short of time and low on supplies? Then this store-cupboard Italian omelette packed with mixed frozen vegetables, eggs and grated cheese is the answer. Serve with bread and butter soldiers and a spoonful of baked beans.

Preparation time 10 minutes
Cooking time 15 minutes
Freezing not suitable
Makes 6 mini frittatas

150g (5oz) frozen mixed vegetables
3 eggs
150ml (¼ pint) formula milk
50g (2oz) Cheddar cheese, grated

1 Preheat the oven to 190°C (375°F), Gas 5. Lightly brush six sections of a deep muffin tin with a little vegetable oil.

2 Add the vegetables to a saucepan of boiling water and cook for 3–4 minutes. Drain and roughly chop, then divide between the sections of the muffin tin.

3 Beat the eggs, milk and cheese together in a bowl. Pour over the vegetables, mix together and then bake in the oven for 15 minutes until well risen, set firm and golden brown. Leave to stand in the tin for a few minutes, then loosen the edges and turn out. Serve warm or cold.

 cook's **tip** Diced leftover cooked potato and just-cooked broccoli also tastes good in this recipe, or try potato, peas and a little chopped mint.

Trout chowder

Trout is readily available as fillets and is surprisingly economical. Mild in flavour and full of nutrients, it's a perfect introduction to fish.

Preparation time 15 minutes
Cooking time 20 minutes
Freezing suitable
Makes 4–5 portions

1 trout fillet (about 175g/6oz)
250g (9oz) potatoes
1 spring onion, trimmed
225ml (8fl oz) formula milk
Half a small bay leaf
75g (3oz) frozen mixed vegetables
50g (2oz) baby spinach

1 Rinse the trout fillet with cooled, boiled water from the kettle. Peel the potatoes, then rinse these and the spring onion with boiled water. Dice the potatoes and finely chop the spring onion.

2 Place the potato and onion in a small saucepan along with the milk and bay leaf. Bring to the boil, then cover and simmer for 15 minutes until the potatoes are tender. Meanwhile cook the trout in a steamer set over a pan of boiling water for 10 minutes until the fish flakes easily. Lift out of the steamer, peel off the skin and carefully check for any bones. Finely chop the fish.

3 Remove the bay leaf, add the vegetables to the potatoes and cook for 3 minutes. Rinse the spinach with boiled water, chop and add to the pan, cooking for 2 minutes until just wilted. Stir in the trout and spoon a portion into a bowl to serve now (checking the temperature before serving), leaving the rest to cool. Spoon into containers, cover and freeze until required.

cook's tip

Accompany this with cooked carrot batons so that your baby has some easy-to-grip finger food to try.

Pastina with creamy tomato and basil sauce

Encourage your baby to try coarser textures by stirring tiny pasta shapes into softly blended Mediterranean vegetables.

Preparation time 10 minutes
Cooking time 19–20 minutes
Freezing suitable
Serves 4–5

1 spring onion, trimmed
150g (5oz) button mushrooms, trimmed
1 stick celery, trimmed
150g (5oz) or 1 courgette, trimmed
350g (12oz) or 5 fresh tomatoes, skinned (see page 136)
1 tablespoon olive oil
Half a small clove of garlic, peeled and finely chopped
2 tablespoons chopped fresh basil leaves
2 tablespoons mascarpone cheese
65g (2½oz) pastina or tiny pasta shapes for soup

1 Rinse the spring onion, mushrooms, celery and courgette in cooled, boiled water from the kettle. Drain and chop. Chop the tomatoes, discarding the seeds.

2 Heat the oil in a saucepan, add the garlic and all the vegetables except for the tomato. Stir fry for 4-5 minutes until softened. Add the tomatoes, then cover and simmer for 10 minutes. Bring a separate saucepan of water to the boil, add the pasta and cook for 5-6 minutes until tender. Drain.

3 Stir the basil and cheese into the tomato sauce. Chop or mash, to suit your baby, then mix in the pasta. Spoon a portion into a bowl (checking the temperature before serving). Spoon the rest into freezer containers. Cover and freeze until required.

cook's tip

If you can't get tiny soup pasta then use whatever you have, cook for slightly longer and then chop it up.

Tiddlers' tagine

For an older baby, try serving this tagine with a spoonful of soaked couscous and a spoonful of frozen peas or chopped green beans.

Preparation time 15 minutes
Cooking time 1 hour 20 minutes
Freezing suitable
Serves 4-5

1 spring onion, trimmed
100g (4oz) carrots, peeled
100g (4oz) parsnips, peeled
175g (6oz) or 1 lean lamb rump steak, all fat removed
4 undyed dried apricots
1 tablespoon olive oil
Half a small clove of garlic, peeled and finely chopped
75g (3oz) tinned, salt-free chickpeas, drained
Large pinch each turmeric, ground cumin, coriander and cinnamon
400ml (14fl oz) homemade vegetable or chicken stock or water
100g (4oz) tinned tomatoes

1 Preheat the oven to 180°C (350°F), Gas 4. Rinse the spring onion with cooled, boiled water. Drain and slice the onion and dice the vegetables. Dice the lamb and apricots.

2 Heat the oil in a flameproof casserole dish, add the lamb and spring onion and stir fry for 4-5 minutes until lightly browned.

3 Mix in all the remaining ingredients, bring to the boil, breaking up the tomatoes, then cover and transfer to the oven. Cook for 1 hours 20 minutes. Chop or mash to suit your baby. Spoon a portion into a bowl (checking the temperature before serving), leaving the rest to cool. Transfer to small freezer containers, cover and freeze until required.

cook's tip

Tinned butter beans, flageolet or haricot beans can also be used in place of the chickpeas. Just make sure that the water in the tin doesn't contain salt. If you're unsure, check the label on the tin.

Cardamom and apricot sundae

Although made especially for your baby, there is no reason why this delicious dessert cannot be served to adults too! If your child seems extra hungry, serve this with a mini rice cake.

Preparation time 15 minutes
Cooking time 10 minutes
Freezing apricot purée only
Serves 3–4

100g (4oz) undyed dried apricots
2 small cardamom pods
150ml (¼ pint) boiling water from the kettle
3 tablespoons freshly squeezed orange juice
1 small ripe banana
100g (4oz) natural bio yoghurt

1 Put the apricots in a saucepan, crush the cardamom pods then add the pods and seeds to the pan along with the boiling water. Cover and simmer for 10 minutes until the apricots are soft.

2 Scoop out the cardamom pods and seeds, then purée the apricots, cooking water and orange juice in a liquidizer until smooth. Leave to cool.

3 Peel and coarsely mash or chop the banana to suit your baby. Stir into the yoghurt, then spoon into four small dishes. Spoon the apricot purée on top, then swirl together with the handle of a teaspoon. Chill until required.

 cook's tip The apricot purée can be frozen in the sections of an ice-cube tray, then defrosted and mixed into a little yoghurt as and when a dessert is required.

Snacks and drinks

Introduce your baby to as many new foods as possible to encourage her to eat a wide variety of things. It might be an idea, however, to leave a day or so between introducing each new food so that if your child does have an adverse reaction, you can identify the cause.

This is also great time for your baby to try the food that the rest of the family eats. Make sure anything you give her is soft and easy to chew, and mince or mash it well. What you offer your child now may influence her eating habits for life. Try to avoid giving her high-sugar, high-fat foods such as biscuits, crisps and cake; instead offer foods that are healthy and nutritious, such as fresh fruit and vegetables and wholegrain cereals.

Healthy finger foods

Pieces of fruit and vegetables (peeled, de-seeded and diced as necessary), breadsticks, crackers and pieces of cheese all make good snacks. You can also try dried fruit such as apricots, dates, sultanas and raisins. These are a good source of iron – vital for your baby's development (see pages 116–19). You may need to soak them in boiled water first, however, as they can be quite tough to chew.

A good phrase to remember is 'Eat the rainbow'. The substances that give fruit and vegetables their bright colours contain vital nutrients. This means that over the course of a day you should serve plenty of different-coloured fruit and vegetables for your baby, such as tomatoes, peppers, bananas, carrots, spinach, oranges, and so on.

Danger of choking

Never give your baby anything with sharp pieces in it, such as fish with any bones left in. Avoid small, hard or round foods such as whole grapes, boiled sweets and nuts. And always stay with your child when she's eating.

Self-feeding

If your baby keeps reaching for her spoon when you feed her, it's probably time for her to try feeding herself. It's vital that you buy soft, non-metal baby utensils, otherwise she could end up hurting herself. Put a plastic mat on the floor and on the table, as you're going to be in for a messy ride. Praise your baby when she uses her spoon but do expect more food to end up on the cat/carpet/walls than in her mouth. For this reason, you should continue to spoon-feed her yourself at times, as well as offering finger foods.

Milk is still important!

Until your baby is a year old, breast milk or formula should remain an important part of her diet. If you want to stop breastfeeding, follow the advice given on pages 125–6. If your baby is less than one year, you should replace breast milk with an infant formula milk. Cow's milk should not be given as a main drink until after her first birthday. Always use whole milk; low-fat and reduced-fat products are not suitable for babies or young children.

Fruit juices and other drinks

From about six months, you can give your baby diluted fruit juice with food (one part juice to five parts water), although it's better to give her cooled, boiled water only. Try to steer clear of citrus juices as these are very acidic and can destroy the enamel on her new teeth. If you buy specially marketed 'baby' drinks, always check the sugar content. Just because they're aimed at little ones, there's no guarantee that they will be low in sugar. Don't be fooled by sugar-free versions of children's medicines either. They will still have sweeteners in them which can be just as damaging to your children's teeth as normal sugar.

When your child gets older, try to discourage her from drinking fizzy drinks. They are full of sugar or tooth-destroying sweeteners and should be kept as a once-a-week treat if you can't cut them out altogether. And try to encourage your child to clean her teeth after drinking one.

Food intolerance and food allergy explained

An allergy is your immune system responding in an abnormal way to a substance or foodstuff that is usually harmless. The immune system overreacts to what it sees as a threat, causing adverse effects in the body. A food intolerance means that your body has an adverse reaction to certain foods and cannot digest them properly. Unlike an allergy, the adverse reaction does not involve the immune system.

If there is a family history of any type of allergy, including hayfever, asthma, eczema or allergy to certain foods, then the risk to your baby of developing an allergy or intolerance is increased. If this is the case, it is important that you talk to your health visitor or doctor about when to introduce certain foods. It is also important not to wean your child before the recommended age of six months.

Foods that are most likely to cause an allergic reaction in babies are: nuts and seeds, dairy products (especially cow's milk), foods containing wheat, eggs, fish and shellfish, and soya.

Gluten intolerance

Gluten intolerance is a sensitivity to the protein gluten, found chiefly in foods such wheat, rye and barley. A small proportion of individuals with gluten intolerance may have coeliac disease, a genetic condition that requires medical management. If there is a family history of gluten intolerance, you should seek advice from your GP. Even if there isn't, it's best to delay the introduction of gluten-containing foods until your baby reaches the age of six months and is better able to digest them. If your baby has gluten intolerance, he may exhibit any or all of the following symptoms:

- Bloated stomach and/or wind
- Skin rashes
- Failure to thrive (not gaining weight or growing properly)
- Loose stools (often foul-smelling) or constipation
- Loss of appetite
- Irritability
- Frequently crying or bringing up food after eating, making 'wet' burping or hiccuping sounds

Lactose intolerance

Lactose intolerance means that the sufferer is lacking an enzyme called lactase which is needed in order to digest lactose, a type of sugar found in milk. The condition is very uncommon in babies. If you suspect your baby may be lactose intolerant, however, watch out for symptoms such as runny stools, wind, spitting up after feeding, colic and crying. If you are at all concerned, contact your GP at once. Babies with lactose intolerance will need to be taken off breast or formula milk straight away and given a special low-lactose formula that is only available on prescription from a doctor.

Nut allergy

Nut allergy is quite rare but the allergic reaction (anaphylactic shock) that the common peanut can trigger is extremely severe. The throat swells and makes breathing incredibly difficult. For this reason, if there is any family history of allergy, including eczema, asthma, hayfever and food intolerance, current government recommendations advise waiting until your child is three years old before trying foods containing peanuts. Bear in mind also that whole nuts do carry a choking risk and should not be given to babies or young children.

Cow's milk allergy

An allergy to a protein found in cow's milk (including cow's milk-based formula) is quite common. Symptoms include stomach pain, vomiting, diarrhoea, eczema and rashes. If your baby shows any of these symptoms following a feed, then seek medical advice. After diagnosing a cow's milk allergy, your GP will find an alternative milk for your baby and give you the appropriate dietary advice. It's estimated that around 12% of babies suffer from milk allergies, although most grow out of it by the age of three. It can be a problem, however, ensuring that your child's diet provides all the nutrients he needs in the meantime.

HOW CAN I TELL IF MY BABY IS ALLERGIC TO COW'S MILK?

The symptoms of milk allergy will vary, but can include anything from eczema and diarrhoea to wheezing and constipation. It usually becomes apparent once your baby is weaned off breast milk and onto a cow's milk-based formula feed, but even breastfed babies can exhibit symptoms if their mother eats a dairy-rich diet. If you suspect that your child may be allergic to cow's milk, consult your doctor.

WHAT ARE THE ALTERNATIVES TO COW'S MILK?

Some children who cannot tolerate cow's milk are able to manage goat's milk, while others are unable to tolerate any kind of milk at all. For those children with an intolerance to all milk and milk products, the best alternative source of protein and calcium is soya-based milk that is fortified with calcium. Several different types of soya milk are available, some with quite a high sugar content, so it's always advisable to check the ingredients first and compare the different brands. Discuss with your doctor how you can ensure that your child's diet doesn't lack the vital nutrients he would otherwise get from cow's milk, such as protein, phosphorus and vitamin D.

TEMPORARY MILK INTOLERANCE

Sometimes, following a gastro-intestinal illness, children who have been happily drinking milk from babyhood can develop a sudden temporary intolerance to milk. Intolerances to food are slightly different from allergies, and the reactions they cause

are generally less severe, with symptoms such as bloating and fatigue. These symptoms may take a while to manifest themselves, and it can sometimes be difficult to tell which foodstuffs are causing the problem.

Milk intolerance is due to the gut becoming temporarily unable to digest the milk sugar lactose (see previous page), causing symptoms such as bloating, diarrhoea, stomach cramps, or sometimes symptoms similar to those of milk allergy except in a milder form. Consult your doctor on how best to cut down on milk in your child's diet. Find out which dairy products don't need to be cut out, so that your child can continue to benefit from the nutrients in them. Certain cheeses and yoghurts are easier to digest than others, and your child may be able to manage these without developing any untoward symptoms. This temporary intolerance should last only a few weeks, and rarely develops into a full-blown milk allergy.

Which foods should I be wary of?

If your baby has allergic tendencies and he eats a food that he reacts against, his immune system will target the food as a foreign body and send histamines to fight it. Histamines are what cause reactions such hives, swelling, eczema, itchiness and wheezing. Allergic reactions typically occur within 24 hours of eating the offending foodstuff. Babies can be allergic to anything, but foods that typically cause a problem include: eggs, cow's milk, peanuts, wheat, soya, 'tree' nuts (Brazils, pistachios, almonds, cashews and walnuts), fish and shellfish. Current recommendations from the government tell us to avoid giving children any foodstuff containing peanuts until they are over three years old.

Introduce each food separately so you know which food is giving your baby a reaction. When introducing any new food, especially when first weaning onto solids, stick to a four-day rule – feeding the food to your baby over a four-day period to see if it causes a reaction. If there is a history of peanut allergy in your family, exclude peanuts from your baby's diet (and from yours when you are pregnant or breastfeeding) until you are sure your baby has not got an allergy to them.

Mum's top tip

I've heard the rumour that some mums give their babies peanuts for the first time outside casualty so if there is a reaction, help is close at hand. I'm not convinced this is the best advice as your child may not have an adverse reaction the first time he eats a particular food yet may experience a reaction the next time he eats it.

What if my baby appears to be having an allergic reaction?

If he can't breathe or his face is swelling up, you need to call 999 immediately since a severe reaction can block the airways and stop him breathing. Similarly, if your baby has severe vomiting or diarrhoea after eating, call 999.

Other reaction such as hives or itchiness should be monitored in case they get worse, but usually a visit to your GP should provide some answers. Your child may be referred to a paediatric food allergist for more tests to discover what he is allergic too.

What food allergy tests will be done?

There are a number of diagnostic tests that can be performed, including blood tests or skin tests in which different foods are placed on your baby's skin to determine which one causes a reaction. If no particular foodstuff can be pinpointed, then an elimination diet may be suggested. You may need to give your baby a limited range of things to eat at first, other items slowly being introduced so that an adverse reaction to any particular foodstuff is easier to spot. A special diet will be drawn up for your baby, depending on his age and what he eats.

Will he be allergic forever?

The good news is about 85% of children grow out of allergies before they go to school. Some will unfortunately be allergic for the rest of their lives, but if they are educated about their allergy, in particular how to avoid the foodstuff in question and what to do in an emergency, it can be managed effectively. Don't forget that some foods are hidden within others (nuts in biscuits, eggs in cakes), so your child will need to be aware of this. Anyone who looks after your child (nursery, grandparent, nanny or babysitter) also needs to be aware of his particular allergy.

Anaphylactic shock

If you are highly allergic to a particular foodstuff, the histamines that your immune system releases can, in some cases, cause a rapid and severe reaction known as anaphylaxis or anaphylactic shock. This generally happens as a result of your body becoming hyper-sensitive to the food after being exposed to it before.

Symptoms usually appear immediately, although they can take between two and four hours to emerge. They can include:

- Severe breathing difficulties (often caused because the muscles in the throat have swollen up)
- Swelling of the lips, face, throat, face and tongue
- Hives
- Dizziness and fainting (probably due to low blood pressure)
- Rapid pulse or irregular heartbeat
- Nausea, vomiting or diarrhoea
- Stomach cramps (this could also be due to food intolerance)
- Skin redness, or looking blue in colour
- Sweating
- Confusion
- Puffiness around the eyes

What foods cause anaphylactic shock?

Any food that causes an allergic reaction can bring about anaphylactic shock, in particular peanuts and other nuts, eggs, milk, fish and shellfish. Wasp and bee stings can cause anaphylactic shock, in addition to some drugs such as penicillin, aspirin, anaesthetics and certain painkillers. Latex can also cause some people to go into anaphylactic shock.

What should I do if my child goes into shock?

If your child is having a severe reaction, immediately call 999. Use an EpiPen (see below) if she has one, but avoid giving her any antihistamines in case she chokes. Lie her down, calm her and reassure her that help is on its way. Loosen any tight clothing. When the paramedics arrive they will usually inject epinephrine into your child to help to relax the muscles in her airway, reducing swelling and increasing blood flow to the brain.

What steps will be taken if my child has a severe reaction?

If your child has a severe reaction, your doctor may recommend she carries an EpiPen, which is a pen-shaped device that carries epinephrine and relaxes the muscles in the airway, reducing swelling and increasing blood flow to the brain. The EpiPen has to be prescribed and it may not be suitable for young infants.

Anyone who looks after your child, including grandparents, friends and teachers, must know how the EpiPen works in case she has a reaction. (They are not always easy to use so make sure your child's carer receives a good demonstration.) She can also wear a bracelet that alerts medical staff to her condition.

How can I help my child?

Try to educate your child about which substances cause her reaction. She may not be aware that nuts can be in biscuits if she can't see them. Get into the habit of checking food labels, asking about dishes in restaurants and washing kitchen equipment thoroughly if you have been cooking with nuts, for instance.

Teething and dental care

Some children are born with a tooth or two, while others can take months for their first teeth to appear. While some babies sail through teething without a care in the world, the majority don't escape so lightly, with painful gums and maybe diarrhoea and tummy upsets caused by the extra acidity in the mouth.

If you baby is about to cut a tooth, she's likely to be irritable, with red cheeks and dribbling more than usual. You may be able to feel the ridge of the tooth just below her gum, which may be red and swollen at this point. Usually, the first teeth to emerge – at around six to seven months – are the four central incisors (two at the bottom and two at the top), followed by four more (at around eight months). Four upper and lower molars then appear (at around 10–14 months), followed by the upper and lower canines (16–20 months) and then four more molars (24–30 months).

If your baby was previously a good sleeper and suddenly wakes up in the night crying, this could also be a sign of teething. If she's putting everything in her mouth (although babies do this anyway whether they are teething or not!) and gnawing her cheeks or fingers, this could also indicate she's about to cut a tooth. Equally, try not to put all the symptoms down to 'teething' whenever your baby seems irritable. Before deciding she must be teething, check first that she isn't ill or simply tired, hungry, windy or bored.

Teething aids and gels

Different types of teething aid are available, from a simple plastic teething ring to teethers filled with gel, which can be cooled in the fridge to ease painful gums, and even special teething toys. Gels that you rub onto your baby's gums can also help ease the pain, as well as homeopathic granules for your baby to 'crunch' against her gums. Giving her something safe to chew on can provide relief from the discomfort as well as distracting her from the pain.

As long as your baby has started to eat solids, and you are watching her while she chews to ensure she doesn't choke, you can try giving her finger food – a bit of toast, for instance, or raw carrot – to help ease the pain. Massaging your finger over the swollen gum may help, although some babies won't let you near their mouths when they are teething. Teething gel can help to temporarily numb the gums, but again it depends whether your baby will let you apply it. Check that the gel is suitable for the age of your baby and follow the instructions carefully, not exceeding the daily dose. If you are breastfeeding, try not to apply it before a feed as it can numb your baby's mouth and make it hard for her to feed.

Comfort and distract your baby – maybe try a change of scenery – to help ease the pain of teething. This can be a great excuse (as if you needed one!) to shower your baby with kisses and cuddles.

 For the **gurgle** video on **How to ease the pain of teething**, go to **gurgle.com** and click on **Videos**

Teething and dental care 171

Looking after new teeth

It's never too early to start thinking about good oral hygiene for your child. As soon as that tiny first tooth makes an appearance, it needs looking after. First teeth usually start appearing at around six to eight months. As with everything, there are exceptions of course. Some children are still toothless at a year. If you're concerned, then take your child to the dentist, who will be able to reassure that, yes, the teeth are there; just not quite through yet.

Some babies manage to cut teeth with no fuss at all, opening their mouths one day to stun you with four pearly-white incisors gleaming in their previously toothless gums. Others fuss and whinge, covering everything around them in drool, until finally, after weeks of sleepless nights, they produce their first tiny tooth.

Bottlefeeding and tooth decay

If you are bottlefeeding, or have moved on to bottle feeds, giving your baby a bottle before she falls asleep can be damaging for those first little pegs. As tempting as it is to give your baby a bottle to help her drop off, it's best to avoid this. If she falls asleep with the teat in her mouth, milk from the bottle will pool around the teeth. Sugar in the formula milk nourishes the bacteria naturally occurring in your baby's mouth, creating tooth-corroding acid. If this happens night after night, it can lead to extensive tooth decay. Baby teeth are much more susceptible to tooth decay, so it pays to be extra vigilant. After every bottle feed, take a damp muslin cloth and gently wipe your baby's teeth and gums. This will help remove plaque and excess sugar.

Your baby's teeth during weaning

When you start to wean your baby, get some rubber-tipped spoons which won't damage your child's gums and new teeth. Babies love to test things in their mouths and may bite down hard every now and then, so metal spoons are a definite no-no. Even before her first tooth has appeared, your baby will be able to chew using just her gums, so when the time's right to move on to not-quite-puréed food, don't worry if it looks lumpy. She can mash it with her gums.

It's also a good idea to get her used to savoury foods, which are, as a rule, less likely to damage her teeth than sweet foods. Giving sweet foods may also encourage your baby to prefer them, a habit that is hard to kick later. A healthy diet means healthy teeth.

- Your baby will probably love naturally sweet vegetables such as peas, carrots and parsnips, but it's important to also get her eating broccoli, cauliflower and potato from the start.

- Small chunks of hard cheese are good for your baby's teeth as they contain calcium.

- Check the sugar content of shop-bought baby food. Glucose, lactose, sucrose and fructose are all just sugar, so look for brands containing less of these.

- Although honey is a natural sweetener, this doesn't mean it's good for teeth and it may encourage a sweet tooth.

- If you give your baby dried fruit (especially raisins) as a snack, bear in mind that they stick to the teeth like glue, so it's best to brush (or wipe) her teeth afterwards.

Mum's top tip

I tried gently cleaning my baby's teeth but it seemed really to frighten and upset her. When I talked to my health visitor, she advised me that it was better to go a few weeks without cleaning her teeth than to risk upsetting her again. She suggested that I try using a soft cloth first to wipe my baby's mouth then gently to wipe 'her lovely little teeth', making a fuss of her. I was to try again in a few weeks with a soft brush.

Teething and dental care 173

Brushing first teeth

So what do you do when those first little pegs appear? Well, most dentists recommend brushing gently as soon as the first tooth is through. Here are **gurgle's** top tips:

- Make sure you buy a toothbrush suitable for the age of your child. You can buy a tiny toothbrush that fits on the end of your finger if your baby doesn't like having a normal one in her mouth.

- Use the tiniest amount of toothpaste and gently brush the tooth.

- It's good to start early to get your baby used to the idea of it being part of a routine. Make toothbrushing one of the last things your baby does before bedtime so that she recognizes that it's part of the routine.

- When your baby is really little, sit her on your lap, pop the toothbrush in her mouth and brush with a gentle, circular motion. Never press hard. Try to brush her tongue a little bit too as this is where lots of bacteria live.

- When your child gets a bit older, let her get involved in choosing a toothbrush (as with most things these days, there are dozens to choose from), and encourage her to stand next to you while you brush your teeth. Let her brush your teeth for you if you like, pointing out how to get to the back and behind your teeth. This should help her have more of an idea of what she should be doing when she cleans her own.

- As soon as your child is old enough to get the concept of spitting out the toothpaste, this should be encouraged. Indeed, toothbrushing should be overseen by you until your child is about seven to make sure she doesn't swallow too much toothpaste or accidentally falls with a toothbrush in her mouth.

top tips

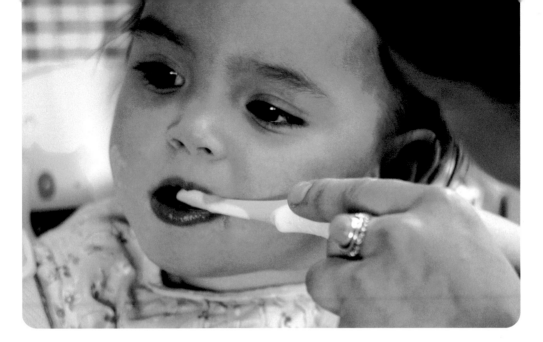

Going to the dentist

Get your child used to the dentist from a young age. She can start going as young as 12 months, and although at this age the dentist can do little more than say: 'Yes, there are teeth in there', the visit will help familiarize your child with the dentist's chair.

- Take your child every year for a check-up. If you don't think your dentist is particularly child-friendly, find one who is.

- If you yourself are scared of the dentist, do everything you can to hide it. Never talk about your dislike of dentists in front of your child, and never moan about a toothache following any dental treatment. Your child will start to think that the dentist causes pain and may not tell you if she has something wrong with her teeth.

- If you are truly terrified of the dentist and can't even walk into the waiting room without passing out (a slight exaggeration, but you get the point!), then ask someone else to take her. A relative or a friend, anyone who can be calm and comfortable with the whole experience.

Feeding your toddler

Your toddler's feeding routine: 12–18 months

At the age of 12 months, your child can enjoy a full and wide-ranging diet. It'll be easier to include him in family meals, although the thrill of practising new skills such as walking (and running away!) might mean he's less interested in sitting down at the table.

The most important thing to remember is not to overwhelm your toddler with food. Remember that his stomach is still unable to cope with an adult-sized meal and therefore small portions and lots of snacks should still be the order of the day. Regular times for breakfast, lunch and supper should be adhered to, in order to create a routine, but a couple of snacks between each meal will be necessary to keep your toddler going.

Eating with the family

When he slows down enough to eat, your child will prefer to eat his meals in company, and eating with the rest of his family makes mealtimes more fun for him. With everybody eating around the table at the same time, you can introduce new foods to your toddler without too much ado. He's much more likely to be receptive to a new food if he sees everybody else eating it.

Even if you can't always plan family meals to coincide with when your toddler needs to eat, do sit with him while he has his meal. This will ensure that he doesn't feel he is missing out on something while he's eating.

The right diet for your toddler

Don't expect your toddler to follow the same diet as you. Young children have different dietary requirements from grown-ups. Like adults, though, your child needs to eat healthily, from a wide source of foods, to set up good eating patterns for later in life.

AVOID TOO MUCH FIBRE

Remember that your child only has a small stomach, with little capacity for the bulky, high-fibre foods such as bread and pasta which you may consider necessary for a healthy diet. This sort of food is difficult for him to digest and, if eaten regularly, could fill him up, leaving no room for the food that can provide enough calories for all the energy he uses.

KEEP UP THE CALORIES

Your child needs far more calories, and hence far more fat, than you do (around 50% of his diet should come from fat), so forget all the advice you've been given about eating a low-fat, high-fibre diet. This applies only to adults. Fat, being high in calories, is crucial for your toddler because he's using up vast amounts of energy. Good sources include dairy produce (including full-fat cow's milk), meat, fish and eggs.

WATCH SALT AND SUGAR

Try not to give your child processed foods such as biscuits, cakes and crisps. These contain large amounts of sugar and salt, which can be damaging to a young child's developing organs and set up unhealthy eating patterns for later on.

FRUIT AND VEGETABLES

Give him a variety of fresh fruit and vegetables. These provide vitamin C plus other vital vitamins and minerals, not to mention fibre (but without being as filling as bread or pasta). If possible, buy organic and seasonal produce (see pages 108–11). It generally tastes better and has a higher nutritional content.

NEW TASTES

Not only is this a good time to introduce new tastes to your child, as he won't reject foods as readily as he may do later, but it will set up good eating patterns for later in life. Just bear in mind that, if you are introducing new foods to your child, you need to keep it to a maximum of two to three new items a week.

LIQUID INTAKE
Eating solid food and using up so much energy will make your child thirstier than ever and it is vitally important that you offer him water to drink at mealtimes and between milk feeds. If the weather is hot, this becomes even more important. Offer your child cooled, boiled water frequently throughout the day.

Some snack ideas

- Raw vegetables often go down well with toddlers. The bright colours are eye-catching and the crunchy textures interesting to chomp on. Although raw is by far the best way to serve them, to provide the maximum nutritional benefit, if you feel you have to cook vegetables then just lightly steam them rather than boiling the life out of them. A piece of crunchy, steamed bright green broccoli is far more appetizing than when it's soggy, wilted and overcooked.

- Fruit cut up into colourful chunks will also appeal to toddlers. Watermelon, banana and apple always go down well, as do grapes and strawberries (but be careful as strawberries can sometimes provoke an allergic reaction – see pages 162–7).

- Try dried fruit such as apricots, raisins or bananas (bearing in mind that they can stick to your child's teeth – see page 173).

- Try giving your toddler unsalted rice cakes or oatcakes with some hummus, either spread on top or as a dip. You may also want to try making different purées which your toddler can eat as a dip with breadsticks.

- Yoghurt, fromage frais and cheese slices are all good sources of calcium and fat, especially if your toddler is fussy about drinking whole milk, although you should encourage him to drink some milk each day.

Mum's top tip

The best advice I can offer is don't give your toddler food 'treats'. If you you give him drinks or snack foods as a reward for eating vegetables, you are actually signalling to him that some foods are preferable to others. This means your toddler will start to see foods such as vegetables as less desirable than foods full of unhealthy levels of sugar and salt.

Menu planner

	Meal one	Meal two	Meal three	Snack ideas
Monday	* Boiled egg and soldiers * Fruit and yoghurt/ fromage frais	* Pasta with tuna, pepper and tomato sauce * Fruit	* Meatballs and creamy mashed potato * Fruit and yoghurt	* Sandwiches with mashed banana * Raw vegetables * Milk and water
Tuesday	* Cereal * Fruit and yoghurt/ fromage frais	* Chicken chunks with white sauce, rice and broccoli * Fruit	* Spaghetti bolognese * Fruit and yoghurt	* Vegetable purée and breadsticks * Cheese on toast * Milk and water
Wednesday	* Porridge with fruit purée * Yoghurt/ fromage frais	* Cheesy pasta shapes with garden peas * Fruit	* Salmon fillet with puréed vegetable sauce * Fruit	* Baked beans on toast * Fromage frais * Milk and water
Thursday	* Toast soldiers with marmite * Fruit and yoghurt/ fromage frais	* Simple Spanish omelette and salad * Fruit	* Fish and vegetable pie * Fruit and yoghurt	* Rice cakes with hummus and raw vegetable fingers * Dried fruit * Milk and water
Friday	* Cereal * Fruit and yoghurt/ fromage frais	* White fish with parsley sauce and peas * Fruit	* Pasta and seasonal vegetables in a tomato sauce * Fruit and yoghurt	* Sandwiches with ham * Apple and pear slices * Milk and water
Saturday	* Scrambled eggs and soldiers * Fruit and yoghurt/ fromage frais	* Couscous with chicken and apricots * Fruit	* Cauliflower and broccoli cheese * Frozen yoghurt	* Baked sweet potato chunks and vegetable dip * Fruit * Milk and water
Sunday	* Eggy bread * Fruit and yoghurt/ fromage frais	* Shepherd's pie * Fruit	* Beef and vegetable casserole * Fruit and ice cream	* Baked beans on toast * Fromage frais * Milk and water

Vitamin supplements

Current government advice is that from six months breastfed babies should be given supplementary doses of vitamins A, C and D. Bottlefed babies who receive 500ml (18fl oz) or less of formula milk each day should also receive extra vitamins. Speak to your doctor or health visitor about what they recommend.

Moving on to cow's milk

From the age of 12 months, cow's milk can be given as a main drink and is an important source of calcium. Giving cow's milk as the main drink before this age has been linked with an increased risk of developing iron deficiency and anaemia.

Once your child begins to drink cow's milk, he should be given full-fat milk until he is five years old. At the age of 12 months, he requires around 600ml (1 pint) a day. Some parents believe that full-fat milk is bad for their children, but as you may recall (see page 180), it's important not to follow the same guidelines for healthy eating for adults when feeding a young child.

The size zero mentality should not be applied to growing children. It is very important for them to receive enough fat to aid their growth and development. Neglecting to provide this type of nutrition could have a detrimental effect on your toddler.

How much salt should my child have?

The NHS has issued the following guidelines for the maximum levels of salt per day recommended for children:

- 0-12 months - less than 1g per day
- 1-3 years - 2g per day
- 4-6 years - 3g per day
- 7-10 years - 5g per day
- 11 years+ - 6g per day

To stay within these guideline amounts, you should aim to:

- Limit salty foods in your baby or child's diet
- Not add salt during cooking
- Limit processed foods, such as ready meals, pies, biscuits, crackers, soup, gravy, sauces, pizza, tinned vegetables, cheese, bacon and crisps, which are all very high in salt.

WHAT TO LOOK OUT FOR ON FOOD LABELS

As your baby grows into a toddler and starts eating more solids, it's important to check the nutritional information on food packaging. Lots of food aimed at children can be quite high in salt. On food labels salt is usually referred to as sodium. If the food contains 0.6g sodium or more per 100g (4oz), it has a high salt content. If it contains 0.1g or less per 100g (4oz), the salt content is relatively low.

Cut down on the number of salty snacks your child has, such as crisps and biscuits, and swap them for low-salt foods. Try dried fruit, raw vegetable sticks and chopped fruit to keep things varied.

WHAT PRODUCTS MIGHT HAVE ADDED SALT?

Foods made specifically for babies, such as food in jars and infant cereals, have a low salt content, as salt is not added during processing. These should not be confused with foods aimed at older children, which can be highly processed and have a high salt content that would be unsuitable for your baby. If you do choose to offer your baby or toddler high-salt foods, the NHS recommends that you offer only small amounts occasionally.

Suitable low-salt foods for your baby include fruit, vegetables and salads, plain meat, poultry and fish, eggs, pulses and milk. Whether they are fresh, tinned or frozen shouldn't make a difference as long as they have no added salt (although tinned vegetables often do have added salt, so be especially careful to check these). Rice and dried pasta are also low in salt – there's no need to add salt during the cooking.

Making mealtimes happy

Few things are guaranteed to cause as much stress in toddler households as mealtimes. The simple act of obtaining nourishment from food can become a fierce power struggle, with parent and child each trying to get the upper hand. But it doesn't have to be like this.

While it's important to try to instil good table manners from an early age, you need to make allowances for your child. If a bit of unintentional mess is the by-product of meals eaten with gusto, it's not worth making a fuss about a little spilt sauce and a few pasta twists on the floor. If your child enjoys hoovering peas up with a spoon, don't insist on her trying to manipulate them into her mouth with a knife and fork. Food is, after all, meant to be fun!

Top tips for happy mealtimes

There are two areas where mealtimes tend to give rise to arguments: what your child is eating, and how she is eating it. Read **gurgle's** top tips on how to encourage good table manners at the same time as making mealtimes easy and fun for everyone.

- Set a good example. Don't get up in the middle of a meal to answer the phone, for example, and don't be tempted to walk around eating or drinking.

- Try and get rid of potential distractions. Turn the TV or radio off, and discourage your child from having toys at the table.

- Mealtimes aren't just functional: eating is also a social activity, and it's no fun doing it alone, especially with someone standing over you and watching. Try wherever possible to have a meal with your toddler, and eat what they are eating.

- Give your toddler some choice in the food she eats, such as a choice of sauces or vegetables.

- If she's a fussy eater, try and make her food interesting; experiment with different arrangements on the plate, making faces or other pictures, and different combinations of colour.

- Try serving food in a different way – cut sandwiches into funny shapes or arrange slices of fruit for her to make a picture with.

- Find food that your child can help you make. Most children love helping to make their own pizza toppings, for example, and enjoy seeing and eating the cooked result.

- Learn to accept that your child has had enough, and when she has, encourage her to ask if she can leave the table, rather than just getting down when she feels like it.

top tips

Fussy eaters

At this stage, don't be surprised if your child suddenly becomes a bit of a fussy eater. Most children go through this phase at some time, and now that yours is a bit older she likes to test the waters by challenging you. It is all part of the push for independence.

That said, this doesn't always make for an easy life and many parents become worried and frustrated when their children refuse food. However, trying to bargain and cajole your toddler to eat is not the best way of solving this issue.

If you believe your child is being stubborn about not eating certain foods, rather than having a genuine dislike for them, you will need to develop certain strategies. The most important thing is to keep your cool. Toddlers love to push their parents, and the attention that refusing to eat incites makes it worth it to them.

It is important to remember that your child won't starve herself. If she is refusing food, take the plate away, but don't offer anything unhealthy in its place. Here are **gurgle's** top tips for combating fussy eating:

top tips

- Make sauces and purées of vegetables that your child professes to dislike and use them on meat, fish and pasta. That way you are still getting important nutrients into her.

- Arrange the food into smiley faces and colourful patterns on the plate.

- Buy sectioned plates with pretty pictures on them.

- Don't bribe your child with unhealthy alternatives.

- Make sure you only give small portions of everything in order not to overwhelm her.

- Make sure you sit down with your child to eat. A busy, distracted parent will be seen as a challenge by a toddler who wants your attention, and lots of it!

- Let her choose some vegetables to put in her meal so that she feels she's part of the process.

- Try and invite other children over for tea. If she spies a friend eating something, she will doubtless want to eat it too.

- Include your toddler in mealtimes. Give her (harmless) items to lay the table with and talk to her about what you are doing to keep her interest and attention.

- Prepare food in advance that can be frozen so you are less likely to be distracted and busy at mealtimes.

- Above all, keep calm and don't respond to tantrums.

Mum's top tip

I worried that my daughter would never, ever eat vegetables. My health visitor said that toddlers often need to be offered something several times before they eat it but that it's worth persevering. In the end, I found the best way round this was to mix vegetables into cheese sauce or make vegetable fritters so she could pick them up to eat them. I also tried roasted vegetables, which she loved, such as carrot, parsnip or sweet potato. These are quite sweet when roasted but are a good source of nutrition all the same.

top tips

Tempting snacks and finger foods

Presentation is often the key to perking up the interest of a toddler. Bright, eye-catching colours and shapes work wonders to focus a distracted child on her food. If you can, buy organic and seasonal fruit and vegetables. They will taste better and be more nutritious. (For more on the benefits of buying organic, see pages 108–11.) Wherever possible, try to prepare meals in advance or have the raw ingredients to hand so that you can get food into your hungry toddler without too much delay!

- Raw vegetable strips such as carrot, celery and cucumber are crunchy and good for gripping with little fingers. Your child will enjoy their bright colours and have fun crunching on them.

- Fruit cut into bite-sized pieces will also appeal to your toddler. Try melon, bananas, pears, apples and grapes. When in season, strawberries are good too (bearing in mind that they can cause an allergic reaction in young children).

- Breadsticks, rice cakes and oatcakes make good finger food. Make different purées for dipping with these. (For some ideas for making purées, see the recipes on pages 130–39.)

- Cut sandwiches into different shapes (using different-shaped pastry cutters), filling them with mashed banana, avocado or tuna fish.

top tips

- Cheese, cut into slices, yoghurts and fromage frais are good sources of fat and calcium for your toddler. You can make fruit smoothies by blending natural wholemilk yoghurt with fresh fruit.

- Offer your child cooled, boiled water frequently throughout the day. (For advice on why water is best, see page 140.)

Your toddler's feeding routine: 18–24 months

By this age, your child's growth rate will have slowed down quite considerably compared to the accelerated period of growth to date. He is also more active thanks to a predilection for charging about the place like a hyperactive hare. Your toddler will probably change shape as he loses his puppy fat, becoming a decidedly different-looking creature from the baby he once was.

However much he has grown, though, the fact remains that your child's stomach still won't be able to cope with very big meals. To keep his energy levels topped up, make sure he has lots of small meals and plenty of nutritious snacks throughout the day. If you can manage to eat together as a family, continue to do so as this helps to build some routine into mealtimes.

Mum's top tip

At 19 months, my son would only eat soft cheese, bread, cereal, yoghurt and fruit. Sometimes he would eat rice or pasta with butter. He wouldn't eat meat, or vegetables, or pasta with sauce. The nutritionist told us that our son would not suffer from poor nutrition and that, in his own time, he would accept a wider range of food. The nutritionist was right: he did come round in the end, but it was good to seek professional advice to put our minds at rest.

Babies grow at an incredible rate; sometimes up to 8cm (3in) in a single month. But this growth rate slows down significantly by the time a child reaches the age of two, at which point it drops to around 8–13cm (3–5in) in an entire year. Even though your child's rate of growth has slowed, it doesn't mean that good nutrition shouldn't remain a top priority. Equally, try not to worry if your child doesn't seem at all keen on eating on certain days – a healthy toddler will never knowingly starve himself.

Encouraging good eating habits

Your toddler will need to eat when he feels hungry. So it's a good idea to have fruit and vegetables ready to whip out before he can protest too much at the gap between his request for food and its arrival.

Toddlers are not the most patient of creatures and preparing food while he is in full-on screaming mode is no fun at all. Bear in mind that fast food does not need to be junk food and that if you keep a scrupulous eye on what foods you are giving your toddler, you will be setting up healthy eating patterns for life.

Little and often is still the order of the day. Most of the foods introduced at 12 months make excellent snacks and don't require much preparation, such as fresh fruit and raw vegetables, sandwiches, toast, bowls of cereal, and dips with breadsticks.

As a rule, encouraging your child to eat a meal in company (even if it's only one other person) at breakfast, lunch and suppertime is a good routine to get into. Other than this, snacking and grazing on healthy foods is perfectly acceptable for a child of this age, helping to buoy up his energy levels throughout the day.

Healthy eating

Your child should be getting a good variety of protein, fat, carbohydrates, vitamins and minerals from his diet. He'll get these by eating a balanced diet of fruit, vegetables, dairy produce, meat, fish, pulses and pasta.

What has no nutritional value are sugary foods, and you should try to steer clear of these. Even if you have managed to restrict such foods in your child's diet until now, he'll become more exposed to them as he gets older and has meals in different households. Other people, such as grandparents or friends, may offer biscuits and cakes as a 'treat', but this should be gently discouraged if possible.

Apart from anything, offering a child a sweet reward or treat could mean he will start to associate other foods with being less desirable. Processed foods often contain dramatically higher levels of salt and sugar than is recommended. They will provide only short bursts of energy, leaving your child, grumpy and tired. In addition, sugary foods cause tooth decay. In a similar vein, it's best to avoid giving sweetened drinks, offering water instead.

Vitamin supplements

Current government advice is that from six months until five years of age, most children should be given supplementary doses of vitamins A, C and D. Speak to your health visitor or doctor about whether they would advocate giving your child a supplementary vitamin. If your child eats well and healthily, then he may not need extra vitamins.

Menu planner

	Meal one	Meal two	Meal three	Snack ideas
Monday	* Toast and spreads * Fruit smoothie (fruit blended with yoghurt)	* Macaroni cheese and broccoli * Fruit	* Spanish omelette with ham and vegetables * Fruit sorbet	* Shaped sandwiches with different fillings * Fruit * Milk and water
Tuesday	* Porridge with soaked apricots and honey * Yoghurt/ fromage frais	* Seasonal vegetable soup with mini pitta pockets to dip * Fruit	* Haddock mornay, petit pois and mashed potato * Frozen yoghurt	* Baked beans on toast with grated cheese * Milk and water
Wednesday	* Cereal with fruit * Yoghurt	* Flaked salmon fillet with steamed broccoli and noodles * Pear quarters and yoghurt	* Polenta slices with vegetable sauce and melted mozzarella cheese * Fruit	* Cheese on toast * Dried fruit * Fromage frais * Milk and water
Thursday	* Scrambled eggs on a split muffin * Fruit salad	* Small baked potato with tuna mayo and pieces of raw tomato and cucumber * Yoghurt	* Spaghetti bolognese with steamed broccoli * Fruit	* Cheese on toast with ham * Fruit * Milk and water
Friday	* French toast or omelette * Fruit smoothie	* Lentil and vegetable soup with a dollop of crème fraîche * Fruit	* White fish and parsley sauce with peas * Fruit and yoghurt	* Rice cakes/ breadsticks with hummus and raw vegetable fingers * Milk and water
Saturday	* Scrambled eggs and soldiers * Fruit and yoghurt	* Shepherd's pie and vegetables * Fromage frais	* Baked sweet potato with filling * Fruit salad	* Raw vegetable fingers and dip * Fruit * Milk and water
Sunday	* Boiled egg and soldiers * Fruit salad and fromage frais	* Homemade pizza with salad * Fruit	* Couscous with chicken and vegetable sauce * Frozen yoghurt	* Baked beans on toast * Fromage frais and fruit * Milk and water

How much food does my toddler need?

The rapid rate of growth your child experienced in the first year of her life will slow down during the second year. Correspondingly, her appetite will diminish.

Additionally, because of her small tummy, she'll need only about a quarter to a third of an adult-sized portion. So if you have two slices of bread for breakfast, your toddler will probably only need about half a slice to fill her up. It can be surprising just how little your toddler does eat, but remember: toddlers are very unlikely to let themselves go hungry. If you have any concerns about how much your child eats, however, speak with your doctor.

top tips

- Offer her three regular meals and two to three healthy snacks a day.

- Remember it's not unheard of for toddlers not to want to eat anything at mealtimes. Letting a child skip a meal is a difficult concept for many parents, but she should be allowed to respond to her own hunger cues.

- Only give snacks when your child is hungry or thirsty, not as entertainment or as a distraction.

- Don't give any more than the recommended 300ml ($\frac{1}{2}$ pint) of milk a day. If your toddler drinks too much milk, she may not want to eat solid foods.

- Offer small servings and let your child ask if she wants more. It's important not to push food on a child who's not hungry. On the other hand, she shouldn't be allowed to eat whenever she wants all the time; some sort of routine is necessary.

Offering a balanced range of foods

When it comes to food, toddlers can test the patience of even the most saintly parent. They are often picky eaters and can display a Herculean-like resistance to trying new food. But there are plenty of ways you can help make sure that mealtimes don't become a battleground. Read on for gurgle's top tips on toddler feeding.

Try to include some of these sorts of food every day in your toddler's diet:

- Milk and dairy products – these provide fat, protein, vitamins and minerals. Up until the age of two, your child should have around 250–300ml (about ½ pint) of full-fat cow's milk daily. Cheese and yoghurt should also be full fat. (For more information on the importance of fat in your child's diet, see page 180.)

- Meat, eggs, beans, lentils and oily fish (sardines, mackerel, tuna – no more than four portions of oily fish a week for boys and two portions a week for girls, see page 206). These are rich in nutrients such as protein, vitamins and minerals.

- Bread, muffins, cereals, rice, noodles, pasta and potatoes – these starchy foods provide fat, vitamins, minerals and fibre.

- Fruit and vegetables – these contain vitamin C and other protective vitamins and minerals, as well as fibre. (For advice on not giving too much fibre to your toddler, see page 180.)

top
tips

Foods to avoid

- Raw eggs and foods containing partially cooked eggs, because of the risk of salmonella.

- Whole or chopped nuts, to eliminate the risk of choking. (Bear in mind, too, that nuts can cause an allergic reaction in some children – see pages 168–9.)

- Shark, swordfish or marlin, because they contain relatively high levels of mercury.

- Raw shellfish, because they can cause food poisoning.

- Food containing high levels of salt, and food and drink containing high levels of sugar.

- Artificial flavourings, colourings, preservatives and sweeteners. These are banned from manufactured baby and toddler foods but can be present in other processed foods. Certain additives have been linked to behavioural problems in children.

- Drinks containing caffeine, such as coffee, tea and many fizzy drinks.

Mum's top tip

My health visitor's advice on vitamin drops was that all children between six months and five years old could benefit from taking drops containing vitamins A, C and D. Vitamin drops are available to buy cheaply from child health centres and are free for children under five years for families receiving income support or an income-based job seeker's allowance. Remember that sunlight is important to boost vitamin D levels but always make sure you protect your child's skin with a good-quality sunscreen.

How much food does my toddler need?   199

Helping your child avoid weight problems

The number of overweight children in the UK is growing at an alarming rate, with around 30% now considered overweight or obese. What's more, children are becoming overweight at an earlier age. Birmingham paediatrician Professor Tim Barrett has recently treated five clinically obese children under the age of four.

Why are more children overweight?

Experts agree that very few children become overweight because of medical problems. Instead, lack of physical activity coupled with poor diet are deemed the main culprits. These days, children spend far too little time engaged in physical activity and far too much in front of the TV, computer or video-game console. According to recent findings by the National Diet and Nutrition Survey, four out of ten boys and six out of ten girls don't do the recommended minimum of one hour a day physical activity.

Add to this the fact that today's busy families have less time to prepare nutritious, homemade meals, plus the abundance of high-calorie, fat-laden confectionery, crisps and snacks ruthlessly targeted at children, and the reasons for the crisis become more apparent.

How can I tell if my child is overweight?

In an average child, 20-25% of the body mass index (or BMI) will be fat, but specialists report some toddlers with up to 50% body fat. However, measuring BMI alone is not appropriate for children as they are still growing. If you are concerned that your child is overweight, seek confirmation from your health visitor or GP, who may then refer him to a dietician.

Is my baby overweight?

Your GP or health visitor is the best person to assess whether your baby is overweight. Never attempt to put a baby or toddler on a diet unless medically supervised. If your GP or health visitor feels that there is a problem, these are the suggestions they may make:

- Avoid grazing if you are breastfeeding. Grazing is when a baby feeds at frequent intervals rather than set times. A baby who grazes could become a toddler or child who comfort eats.

- If are bottlefeeding your baby, don't feed more frequently than every two hours at birth, and every three hours when you baby is two to six months of age.

- Don't keep forcing a bottle on your baby until he's finished every last drop. He'll know how much milk he needs.

- Don't feed your baby whenever he cries, or you will teach him that food relieves stress. Crying could mean your baby is thirsty (in which case, give him cooled, boiled water) or just wants human contact.

- Feed your child slowly. If you are bottlefeeding, don't enlarge the hole in the teat to increase milk flow. Bear in mind that it takes 15–20 minutes for your baby to feel full.

The dangers of obesity

Overweight and obese children risk a number of health problems:

- Increased risk of Type II diabetes, also known as adult-onset diabetes
- Increased risk of high blood pressure
- Trouble with bones and joints
- Sleeping disorders

As your child gets older and he and his peers become more aware of appearances, he may also be exposed to bullying, which could in turn lead to low self-esteem or even depression.

How to help your child

A young child should never be put on a weight-loss diet unless it is under medical supervision. Instead, work to change poor eating habits and to encourage physical activity.

Eating dos and don'ts

Make sure your child eats a balanced diet, incorporating plenty of fresh, nutritious foods and as little processed food as possible.

- **Don't** give your child high-fat, high-sugar snacks such as cake, crisps, chocolate and biscuits. **Do** offer healthy alternatives such as wholegrain bread and cereal, crackers, fresh fruit and vegetables.

- **Don't** automatically reach into the freezer for pre-prepared, processed food for your child's supper. **Do** try to give your child five portions of fresh fruit and vegetables a day.

- **Don't** fry food. **Do** grill or bake food. Oven chips are lower in fat than fried chips, while burgers and fish fingers taste just as good baked or grilled.

- **Don't** give sugary drinks. **Do** give fresh fruit juice diluted with water, or plain water.

- **Don't** let your child skip breakfast, or prepare him a huge fry-up or piles of toast every day. **Do** make sure your child eats a healthy breakfast, such as a wholegrain cereal with milk, plus some fruit.

- **Don't** allow your children to eat in front of the TV, computer or while doing their homework. **Do** encourage the whole family to sit down for meals together, and to take time over those meals.

- **Don't** go to fast-food restaurants when you're out and about. **Do** look for cafés serving, for example, salads or healthy sandwiches.

- **Don't** allow children to graze constantly. **Do** provide three meals with one or two nutritious snacks in between at regular times during the day.

- **Don't** allow your child to bolt his food down because he wants to get back to whatever he was doing. **Do** encourage him to chew more slowly and to really savour his food. This will make him feel more full more quickly, and less likely to overeat.

- **Don't** plonk your child's meals down in front of him every day. **Do** encourage your child to help out in the kitchen whenever possible, involving him in the meal-making process.

Helping your child avoid weight problems

Increasing physical activity

Try to make getting out and about as fun as possible, rather than a chore. Ask an older child what could be more boring than watching other people live their lives on TV, when he could be out there living his own. See opposite for top tips on how to get your child out and about.

- Encourage your child to join after-school clubs and sports activities as much as possible. If he is a toddler, sign him up for a swimming club or gym class – whatever is available in your area.

- If your child goes to nursery or a childminder while you are at work, make sure that whoever looks after him is well aware of your concerns. Ask her how much exercise your child gets during the day and request that it is increased if you don't feel it's enough. Keep an eye on what your child eats there, writing out a list of all the foods you don't want him to be given and firmly requesting that it is stuck to.

- Walk everywhere! If your child's school or nursery is near enough and it's practical, leave the car behind and walk your child there and back.

- Get out and about as a family as much as possible. Jog with your toddler as he cycles along; play badminton in the garden or park, throw a frisbee around or have a kickabout; commit to going swimming once a week.

- Discourage sedentary activity. Be firm about the amount of time your child can spend daily watching TV or on the computer. Encourage him to be selective about what he watches, rather than just slumping down in front of whatever's on the box. Set limits, and enforce them.

Emotional support

Try not to focus too much on the overweight child in the family; instead, take a low-key, 'whole family' approach. Try to avoid using food as treats or rewards. It's best to take the focus off food and provide plenty of attention, cuddles and encouragement instead.

Prevention

Research suggests that children who have been breastfed are less likely to become overweight. Other studies indicate that smoking during pregnancy increases the risk of having an overweight child.

top tips

Your toddler's feeding routine: 24-36 months

From 24-36 months, your toddler will increasingly enjoy eating food that the rest of the family eats, and will be trying out a wide range of new tastes and textures.

Depending on factors such as age, size and how active they are, toddlers need around 1,000–1,400 calories a day. Provide as wide a variety of nutrients as possible in your child's diet, and use your own judgement and cues from your toddler to assess if she is satisfied and getting adequate nutrition.

Remember to give a mix of these sorts of food to your toddler every day:

- Milk and dairy products, which provide fat, protein, vitamins and minerals

- Meat, fish, eggs, beans, peas and lentils, which are rich in nutrients such as protein, vitamins and minerals. You can give boys up to four portions of oily fish a week, including mackerel, salmon and sardines, but it's best to give girls no more than two portions a week. This is because some fish can contain pollutants known as dioxins and PCBs (polychlorinated biphenyls). These can build up in our bodies over time and could potentially interfere with the development of the baby if a girl gets pregnant in the future

- Bread and other cereals – such as rice, pasta and breakfast cereals – potatoes, yams and sweet potatoes; these starchy foods provide calories, vitamins, minerals and fibre

- Fresh fruit and vegetables, which provide vitamin C and other protective vitamins and minerals, as well as fibre.

How much should my toddler eat?

Unless you are concerned that your toddler is putting on too much weight (in which case you should consult your GP), there is no need to limit her food intake. Instead, manage her appetite effectively by keeping to structured meal and snack times: three meals a day and two to three healthy snacks. Children need to eat more regularly than adults, so there should be no more than 3–4 hours between each meal or snack.

Introducing new foods

Food preferences are established early in life, so this is the time to help your child develop a taste for a wide range of healthy things. You can keep broadening her palate by introducing new flavours and textures.

- Try to make the mealtime environment as happy as possible (difficult at times, it's true, but give it your best shot). Children tend to like foods they associate with having fun and in a relaxed environment will be more willing to try something new.

- Encourage your toddler to have a taste of something, but don't force the issue if she won't try it.

- Introduce only one new food at a time, serving it alongside a food your child likes.

- Don't make a big fuss when you present her with a new food. Instead, present it in a calm, matter-of-fact manner.

- Don't pressurize your toddler into finishing the new item of food. Remove anything she hasn't eaten without comment.

- Offer the same food on several occasions. It can take anything up to 15 tries before a child accepts a new food. If she repeatedly says 'No' one day, she might just say 'Yes' on the next occasion the food is offered.

Top toddler feeding tips

- Offer a wide variety of finger foods. This could include chopped-up pieces of fresh fruit and raw vegetables, lumps of cheese, slices of hard-boiled egg, small pieces of bread or crackers, rice cakes and bagels, pieces of cooked pasta and so on – let your imagination run riot!

- Don't over-season food – young children prefer simply prepared foods.

- Encourage one bite to taste but don't overdo the coaxing. Phrases such as 'Eat it all up' can send your toddler into a panic. Never force her to eat anything or you risk creating a life-long dislike of that food.

- Toddlers often ask for the same food day after day. Be patient – this phase won't last long.

- Children learn to eat by watching others, so eat as a family. Switch off the TV. Don't allow distractions such as mobile phones at the table.

- Don't threaten your child with a punishment or a reward for eating something. This rarely works and can actually put your child off the food in question.

- Don't hurry your child. After a reasonable amount of time has passed, remove the plate without comment.

top
tips

Common feeding questions

When can my child start to use a spoon and fork?

Around 18 months, you might like to give your child a spoon and fork to try out. Try to make it fun by taking her shopping and picking her own baby spoon and fork. At first the spoon will invariably be used as a catapult for peas, so make sure you protect the floor around where she eats. Let her play with the spoon and fork first, but show her now and again what they are used for. If you sit around as a family, she will mimic everyone at the table and have more of idea what a spoon and fork are intended for. If you are having problems getting your toddler to eat, see 'Making mealtimes happy' (pages 186-7) and 'Fussy eaters' (pages 188–91) for advice.

Mum's top tip

When I first tried my daughter with a bowl and spoon, she would just throw them both on the floor as soon as I put them in front of her. I tried everything, including suction bowls and a range of different spoons. In the end, I tried her with a weaning fork and fish fingers on her highchair tray (no bowl, plate or spoon). I let her hold the fork when she wanted to, and used a spoon to feed her when she was absorbed in looking at the fork. I repeated this process over a few days, then gradually re-introduced the bowl, the plate, the spoon... We got there in the end!

How can I get my child to eat a proper meal and not just pick at her food?

Some children are naturally pickers and grazers, and the idea of sitting down and eating a full meal is anathema to them. However, even these pickers do not starve, and you may well actually find that they put away much more than you think. The thing to avoid is letting your child pick and snack her way continuously through the day, as this will obviously spoil her appetite at mealtimes. Keep snacks to a minimum, and limit her intake of liquids to just water as fruit juices and milk can make her feel full when she isn't. If your child is a natural grazer, don't force the issue: as long as she is getting a balanced diet, however small the amounts she is taking at any one time, she won't suffer. Try giving her snacks such as raisins, which are healthy, fun to eat and won't spoil her appetite.

When should my child be able to use a knife and fork?

While most children by the age of two are happy with a fork and spoon, using a knife and fork together can take some doing. Try introducing foods which are soft and easy to cut up, or let your child experiment with foods which don't really need cutting up, such as mashed potato, just to practise using the two together. Four is a good age to start encouraging your child to try a knife and fork, but don't force it. It's not worth turning a happy eater into a miserable one just for the sake of mastering the art of cutlery. Obviously giving your child a sharp knife would be a bad idea, so take her shopping and encourage her to choose her own 'toddler' knife and fork for the task.

Your toddler's changeable appetite

Once your child reaches his toddler years, you may find that he becomes much more picky in terms of what he will and won't eat.

Even if as a baby he gobbled up anything you put in front of him, you may find that he now says 'No' to everything. This can be very frustrating for you, but it is a natural part of your child's development; he is asserting his independence. Although you can't force him to eat, there are ways in which you can encourage him to have a healthy, well-balanced diet.

There are other reasons why your toddler might become more fussy when it comes to food. His rate of growth slows down after the age of one and so he doesn't require as much food, relatively speaking. And once he is mobile and running about, his priorities change: he finds other activities far more interesting than eating.

Don't worry if your child appears to be getting choosier. So long as he gets a little of all the important nutrients – protein, carbohydrates, vitamins and minerals – he will be fine, even if his diet appears a bit restricted for the time being. Remember that protein can be found in food such as meat, eggs and cheese. Carbohydrates are contained in foodstuffs such as bread, pasta, fruit and vegetables. Fat can be found in meat, milk, butter and cheese. Vitamin C can be found in fruit, vitamin D in eggs and butter, and iron in meat, bread and certain vegetables.

Top tips on avoiding food fights

- If your child isn't keen on a particular type of food, don't force the issue but try the same food again a few weeks later – you might be pleasantly surprised!

- Offer your child finger food; many toddlers prefer to feed themselves as it gives them a greater sense of independence.

- Don't label your child as fussy, as he will play up to the role.

- Try not to give your child any drinks within an hour of his meals, as this risks him filling up before he's even touched his food.

- Cut down on any snacks between meals.

- Let your child choose what to eat sometimes (within reason!).

- Eat as a family wherever possible, so that your child can mimic your eating habits.

- Children are more likely to eat food they've helped to prepare, so try to cook together when you can.

- If your child won't eat vegetables, try different types and choose a variety of colours as this will help to ensure that he doesn't get bored. Don't get cross if he still refuses to eat his vegetables; you getting wound up will merely make him more likely to rebel.

- If your child is not keen on meat, make meals which use eggs and beans as these are also good sources of protein. Similarly, if he won't drink milk, you could try other dairy products instead, such as cheese, yoghurt and even ice cream (in small amounts!).

top tips

Feeding your toddler

- Don't overload your child's plate, as he may find this offputting. Instead, start off with small amounts of food and present it in an appetizing form – arrange it into funny faces, for example. It's all right to occasionally play with food.

- Don't impose your own food fads or aversions on your child; lead by example. Eat a healthy, balanced diet yourself. Also, if there's something you don't like, it doesn't mean your child will feel the same way. Just because you can't stand the sight of avocado, it doesn't mean that your child won't love it.

- If he drinks a lot of milk, he might feel full and this could be a reason for his reluctance to eat a varied diet. If you suspect this might be the case, try cutting down on the amount of milk he drinks.

- Obviously, the more varied your child's diet, the better, but if he has a firm favourite, such as spaghetti bolognese, this is fine. You can always surreptitiously hide a few vegetables in the sauce!

- Try to stay calm! Easier said than done, but the more wound up you get, the more likely your child is to rebel. Take several deep breaths and remind yourself that he isn't going to fade away if he doesn't always finish whatever's on his plate.

Mum's top tip

One of the hottest tips my best friend gave me was to allow my toddler time to wind down from busy, full-on playing and running around by giving him something quieter to do as the time to eat approached, to help him make the transition to sitting down for mealtimes. I tried to gauge when he would be getting hungry too. I found that letting him complete a quiet activity 20–30 minutes before mealtimes meant he settled better to his food.

top tips

Resources

Association of Breastfeeding Mothers
A charity run by mothers, for all women wishing to breastfeed
0844 412 2949
www.abm.me.uk

BLISS Baby Life Support System
Support for parents of special care babies
0500 618 140
www.bliss.org.uk

The British Dietetic Association
For nutrition advice
0121 200 8080
www.bda.uk.com

Cry-sis
Helpline for parents with crying and sleepless children
020 7404 5011
www.cry-sis.com

Dads UK
The first and only UK helpline for single fathers
07092 391489
www.dads-uk.co.uk

Diabetes UK
For advice on diabetes when pregnant
0207 424 1000
www.diabetes.org.uk

The Food Standards Agency
For up-to-the-minute advice on food scares and recommendations
020 7276 8829
www.food.gov.uk

Gingerbread
Self-help organization for lone-parent families
0800 018 4318
www.gingerbread.org.uk

Home-Start
Provides support and friendship to parents of under-fives
0800 068 6368
www.home-start.org.uk

La Leche League
For breastfeeding help and how to find personal support in your local area
0845 120 2918
www.lalecheleague.org

NCT (National Childbirth Trust)
Offering guidance on pregnancy, birth and parenting
0870 444 8708
www.nct.org.uk

NCT Breastfeeding Line
Open 8am-10pm every day, with trained breastfeeding counsellors who will listen and help you
0300 330 0771

NHS Direct
National helpline offering medical guidance and health information
0845 4647
www.nhsdirect.org.uk

The Soil Association
For information on organic foods and farming methods
0117 314 5000
www.soilassociation.org

TAMBA (The Twin and Multiple Birth Association)
Provides support for families of twins, triplets and more
0800 138 0509
www.tamba.org.uk

The Vegetarian Society
For information on being a vegetarian and vegetarian recipes
0161 925 2000
www.vegsoc.org

Index

Acknowledgements

We would like to thank the **gurgle** experts' panel for their invaluable help in putting together this book. They are: Thirza Ashelford, MA FRSA Principal, Norland College; Alison Brown, registered midwife and registered general nurse; Dr Dorothy Einon, BSc, Phd, child development expert; Fiona Ford, MSc and dietician, co-director of the Centre for Pregnancy Nutrition, University of Sheffield; Eileen Hayes, MSc, BSc, parenting expert, writer and broadcaster; Dr Rob Hicks, MBBS, DRCOG, MRCGP, writer and broadcaster. The publishers would also like to thank Elizabeth Day, parenting consultant.

Text credits

Mervyn Griffiths, MCh, FRCS, 'Do tongue ties affect breastfeeding', *Journal of Human Lactation* (2004), Vol. 20, No. 4, pp. 409-414; Sue Barlow, Terri Damstra, Aake Bergman, Robert Kavlock, Glen Van Der Kraak (ed), *Global Assessment of the State-of-the-Science Endocrine Disruptors: An assessment prepared by an expert group on behalf of the World Health Organization, the International Labour Organization, and the United Nations Environment Programme* (2002); Martin Paterson, Deputy Director General of the Food and Drink Federation, as quoted by the BBC (16 October, 2003); Professor Tim Barrett, Paediatrician, as quoted by the BBC (3 March, 2007).

Picture credits

All images, other than those listed below, have been provided by **gurgle.com**

11 Ian Hooton/Mother & Baby Picture Library; 25 Niderlander; 37 Ventin; 41 Gladskikh Tatiana; 51 Paul Mitchell/Mother & Baby Picture Library; 55 Spring; 63 Angela Spain/Mother & Baby Picture Library; 105 Monkey Business Images; 141 Monkey Business Images; 153 Ian Hooton/Mother & Baby Picture Library; 191 Ian Hooton/Mother & Baby Picture Library; 207 Ian Hooton/Mother & Baby Picture Library.